VIEWPOINTS®
SERIES

✓ **W9-AKB-842**

Girls and Sports

Other Books of Related Interest:

Opposing Viewpoints Series

The Achievement Gap

Education

Male and Female Roles

Sports and Athletes

Current Controversies Series

Homeschooling

Violence Against Women

At Issue Series

Affirmative Action

Are Athletes Good Role Models?

Can Busy Teens Succeed Academically?

The Olympics

The Rising Cost of College

"Congress shall make
no law ... abridging
the freedom of speech,
or of the press."

First Amendment to the U.S. Constitution

The basic foundation of our democracy is the First Amendment guarantee of freedom of expression. The Opposing Viewpoints Series is dedicated to the concept of this basic freedom and the idea that it is more important to practice it than to enshrine it.

OPPOSING
VIEWPOINTS®
SERIES

Girls and Sports

Karen Miller, Book Editor

GREENHAVEN PRESS
A part of Gale, Cengage Learning

GALE
CENGAGE Learning™

Detroit • New York • San Francisco • New Haven, Conn • Waterville, Maine • London

Christine Nasso, *Publisher*
Elizabeth Des Chenes, *Managing Editor*

© 2010 Greenhaven Press, a part of Gale, Cengage Learning.

Gale and Greenhaven Press are registered trademarks used herein under license.

For more information, contact:
Greenhaven Press
27500 Drake Rd.
Farmington Hills, MI 48331-3535
Or you can visit our Internet site at gale.cengage.com

For product information and technology assistance, contact us at

Gale Customer Support, 1-800-877-4253
For permission to use material from this text or product, submit all requests online at www.cengage.com/permissions

Further permissions questions can be emailed to permissionrequest@cengage.com

Articles in Greenhaven Press anthologies are often edited for length to meet page requirements. In addition, original titles of these works are changed to clearly present the main thesis and to explicitly indicate the author's opinion. Every effort is made to ensure that Greenhaven Press accurately reflects the original intent of the authors. Every effort has been made to trace the owners of copyrighted material.

Cover photograph © 2009/JupiterImages.

LIBRARY OF CONGRESS CATALOGING-IN-PUBLICATION DATA

Girls and sports / Karen Miller, book editor.
    p. cm. -- (Opposing viewpoints)
    Includes bibliographical references and index.
    978-0-7377-4811-6 (hardcover)
    978-0-7377-4517-7 (pbk.)
    1. Sports for women--Juvenile literature. I. Miller, Karen, 1973-
    GV709.G26 2010
    796.082--dc22

                                                      2009028943

Printed in the United States of America
1 2 3 4 5 6 7 13 12 11 10 09

Contents

Chapter 3: Do Schools Support Girls' Sports Programs?

Chapter 4: What Are the Cultural Implications of Girls' Participation in Sports?

Why Consider Opposing Viewpoints?

> *"The only way in which a human being can make some approach to knowing the whole of a subject is by hearing what can be said about it by persons of every variety of opinion and studying all modes in which it can be looked at by every character of mind. No wise man ever acquired his wisdom in any mode but this."*
>
> *John Stuart Mill*

In our media-intensive culture it is not difficult to find differing opinions. Thousands of newspapers and magazines and dozens of radio and television talk shows resound with differing points of view. The difficulty lies in deciding which opinion to agree with and which "experts" seem the most credible. The more inundated we become with differing opinions and claims, the more essential it is to hone critical reading and thinking skills to evaluate these ideas. Opposing Viewpoints books address this problem directly by presenting stimulating debates that can be used to enhance and teach these skills. The varied opinions contained in each book examine many different aspects of a single issue. While examining these conveniently edited opposing views, readers can develop critical thinking skills such as the ability to compare and contrast authors' credibility, facts, argumentation styles, use of persuasive techniques, and other stylistic tools. In short, the Opposing Viewpoints Series is an ideal way to attain the higher-level thinking and reading skills so essential in a culture of diverse and contradictory opinions.

In addition to providing a tool for critical thinking, Opposing Viewpoints books challenge readers to question their own strongly held opinions and assumptions. Most people form their opinions on the basis of upbringing, peer pressure, and personal, cultural, or professional bias. By reading carefully balanced opposing views, readers must directly confront new ideas as well as the opinions of those with whom they disagree. This is not to simplistically argue that everyone who reads opposing views will—or should—change his or her opinion. Instead, the series enhances readers' understanding of their own views by encouraging confrontation with opposing ideas. Careful examination of others' views can lead to the readers' understanding of the logical inconsistencies in their own opinions, perspective on why they hold an opinion, and the consideration of the possibility that their opinion requires further evaluation.

Evaluating Other Opinions

To ensure that this type of examination occurs, Opposing Viewpoints books present all types of opinions. Prominent spokespeople on different sides of each issue as well as well-known professionals from many disciplines challenge the reader. An additional goal of the series is to provide a forum for other, less known, or even unpopular viewpoints. The opinion of an ordinary person who has had to make the decision to cut off life support from a terminally ill relative, for example, may be just as valuable and provide just as much insight as a medical ethicist's professional opinion. The editors have two additional purposes in including these less known views. One, the editors encourage readers to respect others' opinions—even when not enhanced by professional credibility. It is only by reading or listening to and objectively evaluating others' ideas that one can determine whether they are worthy of consideration. Two, the inclusion of such viewpoints encourages the important critical thinking skill of objectively evaluating an author's credentials and bias. This evaluation will illuminate an author's reasons for taking a particular stance on an issue and will aid in readers' evaluation of the author's ideas.

It is our hope that these books will give readers a deeper understanding of the issues debated and an appreciation of the complexity of even seemingly simple issues when good and honest people disagree. This awareness is particularly important in a democratic society such as ours in which people enter into public debate to determine the common good. Those with whom one disagrees should not be regarded as enemies but rather as people whose views deserve careful examination and may shed light on one's own.

Thomas Jefferson once said that "difference of opinion leads to inquiry, and inquiry to truth." Jefferson, a broadly educated man, argued that "if a nation expects to be ignorant and free . . . it expects what never was and never will be." As individuals and as a nation, it is imperative that we consider the opinions of others and examine them with skill and discernment. The Opposing Viewpoints Series is intended to help readers achieve this goal.

David L. Bender and Bruno Leone,
Founders

Introduction

> *"You shouldn't just work on your jump shot. You should work on being a better person, a better teammate, and a better friend."*
>
> —Sue Wicks, Women's National Basketball Association New York Liberty player, Gball Online Magazine: Q & A, 2001.

In the 2008 summer Olympics in Beijing, China won its first team gold medal in women's gymnastics. Two members of the team, Jiang Yuyuan and He Kexin, were accused of being too young to compete; the minimum age for participation is sixteen years old. Although both girls presented passports to the International Olympic Committee (IOC, the governing body of the Olympics) that indicated they were old enough, older documents were unearthed online that put their ages at as young as fourteen. The IOC accepted the passports as official proof that the gymnasts were old enough to participate, and the team competed intact. Regardless of age, the team gave a champion performance, its members impressing the global audience and judges with their skill.

Elite gymnastics has become a sport for girls rather than women. The last fully grown adult female to win an Olympics gymnastic event was Czechoslovakian Vera Caslavska, age 26, in 1968. In 1972, seventeen-year-old Olga Korbut took the gold medal, and the age of women's gymnastics champions has hovered around that mark ever since. Korbut astonished the world with her innovative routine on the uneven bars; video of the event includes ABC network commentators Jim McKay and Gordon Maddox gasping at her performance.

"Has that ever been done before by a girl?" sports journalist McKay wonders aloud. "Not by any human being!" gymnastics analyst Maddox answers.

It is no accident the sport of women's artistic gymnastics was changed by a teenager. Adolescent girls' bodies are leaner and more muscular, without the broad hips and larger chests adult women develop. In the October 2006 publication of *Proceedings: International Symposium for Olympic Research*, Kevin Wamsley and Gordon MacDonald, authors of "Child's Play: Decreasing Size and Increasing Risk in Women's Olympic Gymnastics," describe how the standards for championship-level gymnastics have risen: double somersaults and triple twists have replaced the single versions from competitions in the 1970s and 1980s. Series of moves have become more complicated and difficult, and even the equipment has changed dimensions. The sport now favors the more flexible, lighter, shorter bodies of girls. Furthermore, as competitors get smaller, the standard measures of skill become more extreme. The girls who win are smaller and lighter—and younger—than their competitors and can twist and turn higher and more often. Younger athletes perform a more acrobatic sport. The guidelines for scoring and the intensity of competition in the 2008 Olympics would be unrecognizable to the competitors of the 1954 Olympics, when the sport first appeared in its modern form.

It is a coincidence that the Russian Olga Korbut competed in the Olympics the same year that the United States passed the Title IX legislation requiring equal access to sports in schools for girls. Still, Korbut's achievement had no less impact than that groundbreaking law. The young gymnasts of her generation were a symbol of how girls are important to sports, as participants and as influencers. When they are given the chance to compete as frequently as their male peers are, girls find new ways to play sports, transforming what it means to be a champion as well as finding strategies and techniques adapted to female bodies and new ways of interacting with teammates.

Consider women's basketball. Girls and boys play basically the same game (with a few exceptions), but the women's game is described by coaches and sports writers everywhere as "pure." Men's professional basketball is full of celebrities who are more famous as individuals than as members of a team. Women's teams, however, are famous as teams, and women's games are lauded as displays of athleticism and strategy and fundamental expertise. Women's soccer teams are held in the same regard. Outside of game play, girls are even considered to be more sportsmanlike than their male athletic peers; a 2007 survey conducted by the Josephson Institute, "What Are Your Children Learning? The Impact of High School Sports on the Values and Ethics of High School Athletes," revealed that girl athletes are far more likely than boy athletes to believe that cheating is unacceptable, that it is more important to be a good sport than to win, and that winning is not the only enjoyable part about playing sports. As these girl athletes mature into adult athletes and role models on the national stage, they present to boys and girls alike a vision of the power of sports to transform individuals and improve lives, a vision that stands in stark contrast to the images of famous male sports figures caught up in crime, drugs, and other scandals.

The presence of girls in sports for the past few decades has turned the sporting world into something new. As with all things new, society has to adapt to the changes wrought by the suddenly diverse organizations of girls and women with their own ideas about what sports are for and what they can do. *Opposing Viewpoints: Girls and Sports* explores some of the ramifications of females populating—in great numbers—the ranks of traditionally male pursuits. Its four chapters, How Does Gender Influence Sports Participation? How Does Sports Participation Affect Girls' Health? Do Schools Support Girls'

Sports Programs? and What Are the Cultural Implications of Girls' Participation in Sports? identify many of the current conflicts and triumphs of girls' sports programs and provide a variety of perspectives on what girls participating in sports means to girls, to sports in general, and to the rest of Western society.

 OPPOSING
VIEWPOINTS®
SERIES

 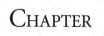

CHAPTER 1

How Does Gender Influence Sports Participation?

Chapter Preface

On October 9, 2008, the *New York Times* reported on a Women's Sports Foundation study that found girls in urban neighborhoods and from immigrant families are much less likely to participate in sports than their suburban or native-born counterparts. Although suburban girls more or less participate in sports at equal rates to suburban boys, urban and immigrant girls lag far behind their male peers, in terms of participation both on organized teams and in physical education classes.

The Women's Sports Foundation survey did not specifically address cultural reasons for the disparity between urban and suburban girls' sports participation. Racial and ethnic categories—particularly conformity to traditional gender roles—could play a part in decisions girls make about athletic pastimes, but these categories represent broad swaths of people who cannot be expected to hold a single opinion about any particular topic or to behave in similar ways. The unequal distribution of girls and boys in sports programs could just as easily have a logistical or environmental origin.

Urban and suburban school districts have very different administrative problems. Cities are by definition densely populated places, with fewer open spaces where children can informally gather and play the games that evolve into team sports as they get older. Urban schools and communities have sports fields, certainly, but the larger populations they serve mean tighter restrictions on availability. Children and teenagers do play sports in the cities, but they have less opportunity to choose for themselves what they like—adults (parents, coaches, and recreation center administrators) often plan for them. Practice spaces at secondary schools are as constrained as the public facilities off campus. With most sports time corralled into organized activities, participants are less likely to discover their talents and interests in noncompetitive, no-stakes settings, and they are less likely to have time to experiment with different games.

Money to provide students access to many different sports is generally less available to urban schools, too. In many places, schools are funded by property taxes; because suburban residences take up more land than those of city dwellers, property-tax revenues are greater in the suburbs, and suburban schools tend to have more money to fund extracurricular activities. Many suburban schools offer a variety of sports teams for boys and girls, even if only a few players are interested. When money and space are at a premium, schools are forced to prioritize, so they choose to support the teams and activities that have a long record of high participation and student interest, and they let the members of other teams fend for themselves.

Despite these restrictive circumstances, urban boys still find ways to participate more than urban girls. The same cultural and media stereotypes about female athletes being unfeminine are delivered to girls in the cities and in the suburbs, but suburban girls—who have more access to time on the fields—don't drop out of sports. It is unlikely that urban girls are so different from suburban girls that they have vastly different interests in sports. It also seems unlikely that, decades after the passing of Title IX and other legislative acts to ensure girls' access to sports programs, school and sports administrators would have the desire or the ability to deliberately deny girls the chance to play. It remains a challenge, however—particularly in urban settings—to continue to develop girls' interest in and protect their access to sports.

The following chapter explores how gender affects girls' sports participation once they decide to play. The authors examine the ways in which girls conform to or disrupt social and physical expectations about their athletic interests and how they identify themselves as girls, as athletes, or as female competitors.

> *"Where height, weight and skill levels allow, there is no physiological reason why girls and boys should not be allowed to play on the same team."*

Girls Should Be Allowed to Play on Boys' Teams

Kris Lines

Kris Lines is head of sports law at Staffordshire University in the United Kingdom and a British gymnastics coach and assessor. In the following viewpoint, he analyzes a ruling of the English Football Association (FA) that bars girls from playing football (soccer) with their male teammates once they reach the age of twelve. Lines examines the reasoning behind the FA's rule and its relationship to the laws about girls and sports. He also compares it to arguments in favor of letting girls play on teams with boys, even when girls' teams are available.

As you read, consider the following questions:

1. What is the official English Football Association ruling about the ages when children may play on mixed-sex teams?

Kris Lines, "Who Says Girls Can't Play on the Same Team as Boys?" *Education Law Update*, October 2006. Reproduced by permission of the author.

2. According to the author, in what way is the Football Association acting legally by barring girls over the age of 12 from playing on boys' or mixed-sex teams?

3. According to Lines, what are the policies in some other countries regarding girls playing on mixed-sex teams?

Minnie Crutwell is a 10-year-old girl from South London who plays football for the Balham Blazers. In March 2006, she reignited the debate over whether girls should be allowed to play football in mixed teams after they had reached the age of 12.

Although Minnie wants to continue playing with her teammates when she turns 12, the Football Association [FA] rules require that she play for a girls' team.

The FA rule reads: 'Save for matches in a playing season in the age ranges under 7, under 8, under 9, under 10 and under 11, players in a match must be of the same gender.'

Minnie responded to the FA requirement by writing to the culture, media and sport secretary Tessa Jowell (who is also minister for women). After going down to London to watch Minnie and her team play, Tessa Jowell arranged a meeting between Minnie and the Football Association to discuss the rule.

Minnie and her coach later submitted written evidence to the select committee on culture, media and sport about women's football.

This [article looks] at the implications of LTAD [long-term athletic development, a British athletic training model] for gender, in particular for mixed-sex activities before, during and after puberty.

In particular, this article will discuss the implications of the recent and controversial case of Minnie Crutwell, the girl who wanted to continue playing mixed football after she reached the age of 12. Although Minnie's case focused on the playing of mixed football, the arguments made and the physiological evidence apply equally to other sports.

Just a Small Piece of the Puzzle

This article will not express a view on whether single-sex or co-educational sport is the better approach to physical education at school. This is an emotive topic and there are advantages and disadvantages to both approaches.

What this article will evaluate is whether girls and boys can play legally on the same team. Religious belief, peer-group pressure, maturity, sexual identity, resource constraints, the nature of the sport, the type of activity, and the confidence of the pupils concerned, will all play a part in the decision. The evaluation offered in this article is, therefore, only a small piece of a large puzzle. . . .

Sex Discrimination

The Sex Discrimination Act 1975 (section 44) says: 'Nothing in Parts II to IV shall, in relation to any sport, game or other activity of a competitive nature where the physical strength, stamina or physique of the average woman puts her at a disadvantage to the average man, render unlawful any act related to the participation of a person as a competitor in events involving that activity which are confined to competitors of one sex.'

Given that the FA believes that the physical strength, stamina and physique of the average female footballer puts her at a disadvantage compared to the average male footballer, there is nothing illegal or discriminatory in the FA's ruling.

Section 44 would allow schools to have separate boys' and girls' sports teams for some sports. Lessons could also be separated into single-sex classes if the sports were of a competitive nature and staff thought that there was a risk of injury through mismatching.

The FA Argument

Effectively the FA argued that its regulations preventing 12-year-old girls from playing on boys' or mixed teams, were for the girls' own good. It pointed to the fact that it has a duty of care to provide safe football for all, and that boys and girls of over 11 are at different developmental stages, and therefore at increased risk of injury if they play together.

The FA also suggested that by segregating the sexes, it would enable women to develop their own teams and identify specific career paths.

These all seem sensible suggestions, but does the evidence support them?

The Physiological Evidence

While it is true that there are certain important physiological differences between girls and boys, this should not be the determining factor when judging whether it is appropriate for them to play in mixed teams. Pre-puberty (LTAD 'fundamentals' stage), although girls generally develop coordination skills faster than boys, there is no physiological reason to justify separating girls and boys in sport.

Girls begin their growth spurt earlier and reach a maximum growth rate at, on average, 11. By contrast, boys reach their maximum growth rate at about 14. Owing to the male hormone androgen, boys develop more muscle mass than do girls. Where a boy and a girl are the same height and weight, the boy will have more fat-free mass (a greater percentage of his body will be muscle) than the girl. So the boy will be stronger, able to run faster and throw farther.

What you would expect to see, therefore, is girls who are faster, stronger and taller than boys at the earlier stages of puberty, with boys becoming faster, stronger and taller later on.

It is obvious then that an unmonitored grouping of 12 to 15-year-old pupils in same-age, co-educational PE [physical

Eri Yoshida: Female Sports Pioneer

The 16-year-old knuckleballer will be the first woman to play on a professional baseball team, after being drafted by Japan's Kobe 9 Cruise on Nov. 17 [2008]. Cynics have suggested the pick was a publicity stunt by the team, part of the country's new Independent League. But the manager who picked Yoshida said he did so because of her formidable sidearm knuckleball, which Yoshida has said she modeled after pitcher Tim Wakefield of the Boston Red Sox.

Time, *"Eri Yoshida,"*
Top 10 Female Sports Pioneers. *www.time.com.*

education] classes could result in physiological mismatching. But balanced against this is the girls' increased physical maturity post-puberty, which could compensate for the increased muscle mass of boys in their peer group.

The Women's Sport Foundation was, therefore, correct in its evidence to the commons culture, media and sport select committee that a ban on 11-year-old girls playing on the same team as boys is an arbitrary barrier.

Not every girl will be able, or want, to play on boys' sports teams. But where height, weight and skill levels allow, there is no physiological reason why girls and boys should not be allowed to play on the same team past a certain age.

If the FA accepts this recommendation, this would place the duty of care firmly on the individual coaches and teachers to ensure that the players were evenly matched and not at any additional risks. While this will be a higher burden to meet, it should also be a more equitable one, which will allow talented older girls to flourish in the sport.

The Position Abroad

There is evidence that this blanket ban on mixed football after 11 is not shared with other countries.

Dutch women's football already profits from a thriving domestic system and infrastructure. Girls can play mixed football with boys until the age of 19—and the number of young females in clubs at all levels is growing. In Germany, girls play in boys' teams for as long as they want to. When they hit the point that they are too slow or are becoming out-muscled, they join a girls' team.

Title IX in America allows girls who wish to participate on boys' teams, the opportunity to do so.

Studies suggest that, owing to the greater demands on them, girls develop technical knowledge and ability at a faster rate when playing in mixed teams than they do when playing in single sex-teams. Having to win their place on a team therefore makes them more competitive.

> *"Because of the perception that boys would hurt or intimidate girls with their superior size, strength, speed, and aggressiveness, many feared that coed field hockey would result in fewer female players."*

Boys Should Be Allowed to Play on Girls' Teams

Sarah K. Fields

Sarah K. Fields is an assistant professor in sport humanities at Ohio State University in Columbus. As a child, she was the only girl on a second-grade soccer team in St. Louis, Missouri. The following viewpoint is excerpted from Female Gladiators, *the first book to examine legal and social battles over the right of women to participate with men in contact sports. A particularly vehement debate has accompanied boys' desires to play on girls' field hockey teams, in part because of the question of whether field hockey is a contact sport, in which larger boys might have an advantage over even highly skilled female players. Fields acknowledges the complexities of the debate but concludes that boys should be allowed to play on girls' teams for the same reason as the converse: fairness and equity require it.*

As you read, consider the following questions:

1. As the author reports, how were courts interpreting Title IX legislation in the late 1970s when boys were petitioning to join girls' teams because no boys' teams were available?

2. Why is the question of whether field hockey is a contact sport so relevant to the debate about whether boys should be allowed to play on girls' field hockey teams, according to the author?

3. What underlying assumption does Fields assert influences legal and cultural conversations about the presence of boys on girls' sports teams?

When the issue of allowing boys to play on girls' teams was first addressed in the courts, the question was extremely broad: Was it legal to permit girls to play on boys' teams but prohibit boys from playing on girls' teams? After Title IX enforcement regulations were enacted in 1975, and in the enthusiasm created by adoption of the [Massachusetts] equal rights amendment, the Massachusetts Interscholastic Athletic Association (MIAA) announced that any child could play on any sports team so long as no separate-gender team existed. That ruling allowed girls to play football and boys to play field hockey, softball, and volleyball.

In 1978 the Newton South [Mass.] High School softball team seemed likely to win the state softball championship, concluding a successful season that many in the state credited to the presence of two boys on the team. The Massachusetts Division of Girls and Women's Sports filed suit against the MIAA to change the rule and keep boys off girls' teams in order to protect athletic programs for females. The next year the MIAA bowed to social pressure and excluded male players from female teams (although female players could still play on male teams) in order to have the lawsuit dropped. Three schools, however, had already placed boys on volleyball teams before the rule change, and the MIAA refused to grant them waivers to allow them to compete. Frustrated, the schools asked the state attorney general to examine the MIAA's rule. He believed it to be a violation of the state's equal rights amendment and filed suit to change the rule. The state's highest court agreed with the attorney general and ordered the rule removed from the books, which allowed boys to play on girls' teams if no comparable boys' team existed. . . .

[The] first Massachusetts decision regarding boys and field hockey, published in 1979, reflected the ideology of gender equality and equal rights feminism that had inspired the ERA [Equal Rights Amendment, which had significant support but never became an amendment to the U.S. Constitution] and Title IX. The court was consistent in refusing to treat boys and girls differently when it came to supporting their athletic aspirations and in rejecting stereotyped assumptions about the children's capabilities. Regardless of whom the MIAA wanted to exclude from which sports (girls from football or boys from field hockey), the MIAA made the same arguments based on the same assumptions: Because boys were bigger, stronger, and faster, girls would be injured and quit playing sports. The court rejected those arguments as being overbroad, paternalistic generalizations and ordered all sports opened to all children, either in the form of separate or coed teams. The court seemed to believe that opening all sports to all children would best protect individuals as well as boys and girls as a class, emphasizing that the purpose of school sports was to maximize participation by all. This sense of openness and equal opportunity, however, would not be the typical field hockey decision. . . .

Skirted Uniforms and Physical Contact

In essence, the courts addressed two basic issues, whether field hockey is a contact sport and whether allowing boys to play undermines girls' athletic programs. Public discourse added one other question: Does the presence of boys in field hockey undermine their masculinity? Even the question of contact was most culturally relevant in relation to questions about physical differences between boys and girls and issues of safety.

These debates were similar to those raised in all contact sports cases. Questions of the legitimacy of the sport itself, of participants' safety, and of what it means to be gendered in sports in America were recast in the battle over field hockey. Now, however, the liberal feminist argument of inclusion— that supporting separate athletic programs for girls is imperative to achieving gender equality—resulted in exclusion. The noble goal of saving girls' sports was premised on the previously villainized paternalistic assumptions that boys are essentially better athletes; that boys are bigger, stronger, and faster than girls; that girls will be injured playing with boys; and that girls will be intimidated by male players and quit the sport. Media reports on coed field hockey were filled with arguments for both sides, and opponents tried an added element of social control by shaming boys away from a sport in which participants wear skirts. . . .

In field hockey cultures, most people seemed to agree that protecting girls' athletic programs is a laudable goal. Although the issue of whether field hockey is a contact sport was relevant to legal arguments surrounding the applicability of Title IX, socially the problem of contact was more connected to protecting girls' sports. Questions about physical differences between boys and girls, safety, and intimidation became particularly relevant. Noncontact sports are by nature less dangerous than contact sports. Fewer catastrophic injuries, for example, occur in tennis than in football. Size and strength are less of an issue because a larger player cannot intentionally use that size and strength to physically harm an opponent. Therefore, the public is less concerned with coed noncontact sports; no one, for example, worries about the physical dangers of coed golf teams. Contact sports, however, do raise the collective eyebrow when teams are coed, in part because size and strength and gender become factors during a game and in terms of safety. Therefore, the struggle over field hockey, both in the courtroom and American societies, began with the question of contact.

The issue of whether field hockey is a contact sport has been highly subjective. Even courts in the same jurisdiction have disagreed on the matter. In [a] New Jersey case, for example, the administrative law judge [ALJ] and the New Jersey court looked at the same witness testimony and reached opposite conclusions. The ALJ concluded that contact is incidental in field hockey, and the court concluded it is a major part of the game. The ALJ let the boy play, and the court did not. The debate stemmed from the inherent contradiction between the rules of field hockey and the realities of the way the game has been played.

Those who have concluded that field hockey is a noncontact sport focus on the literal language of the rules prohibiting contact. Those with the opposing view have cited the course of play itself. Elizabeth Beglin, a former Olympic field hockey player and former coach of the University of Iowa team, has suggested that field hockey is parallel to basketball. Contact has been against the rules, but it has occurred constantly and has only infrequently been penalized. Beglin believes that if basketball is considered a contact sport then field hockey should be as well. Other coaches have submitted affidavits in different cases and used the same analogy, also made by a concurring judge in [a] Pennsylvania case. Similarly, in excluding boys the judge in [a] Rhode Island federal court case relied heavily on the testimony of a high school coach who stated that contact does occur despite the rules against it, especially among novice players or with poor officiating. Further, the coach suggested that contact from sticks and flying balls is frequent. She emphasized the required safety features like shin guards and mouth guards to support her argument.

If field hockey is a contact sport, that would imply that bigger, stronger, faster players would likely have more success. Because boys have those traits, they would be better field hockey players than girls and would therefore take over a team. . . . Viola Goodnow, who coached field hockey for forty years but never coached a boy, said, "If you have a male on the team, he's obviously going to get a spot, because he's quicker, faster, and stronger."

Assumptions of Athletic Superiority

In the media, however, the most repeated concern was not that more athletically gifted boys would take over a team. Rather, people opposed to coed field hockey warned that girls would be injured if boys were on the field. People assumed that boys would not just be larger than girls but somehow more predatory than females who played. An athletic director, for example, argued that having boys on a team would be dangerous: "I have a freshman daughter on the team, and [the boy who wanted to try out] weigh[ed] about 175 pounds. As a parent, I don't know if I would want him swinging a stick next to my 130 pound daughter." The director did not specify if he would discourage his daughter from playing with 175-pound females, implying that size alone was not enough to concern him but gendered size—size enhanced by testosterone—would. . . .

A coach of a single-sex female team that played coed teams pronounced that boys who played field hockey "play on the edge, like they think they're playing street or ice hockey. They throw elbows and push. We're talking about boys that are much bigger than the girls. It isn't fair." No mention was made of the fact that such contact is technically illegal and pushing and elbowing can be penalized by the referees. The concern seemed not so much about the unfairness of the size differential but the unfairness of the difference in perceived attitude between male and female players. Playing a bigger, stronger, faster girl was one thing, but playing a bigger, stronger, faster boy would be another, these coed opponents suggested, because of how the boy would use those physical attributes. The implicit argument was that the aggressive male culture of sport would overwhelm the more supportive female culture of sport.

The result of physical differences and concerns about injury and attitude, those who favored single-sex field hockey maintained, would be that girls would quit the sport or refuse to play with or against boys, hence undermining athletic programs for females. Massachusetts, the one state in the country that mandated the possibility of coed field hockey, was asked at the 1987 New Jersey trial to comment on the results of its experience, which MIAA executive director Richard Neal called a "disaster." He claimed that the presence of twenty to thirty boys in Massachusetts field hockey leagues from 1979 to 1987 had displaced at least some girls from a sport in which they had previously participated. He also testified at trial that an unknown number of girls had quit rather than risk injury of playing against boys and that the same fear of injury had limited the playing opportunities of teams that chose to forfeit rather than play a coed squad. Even girls on the coed team lost playing chances when their opponents forfeited. Because of the perception that boys would hurt or intimidate girls with their superior size, strength, speed, and aggressiveness, many feared that coed field hockey would result in fewer female players.

Inherent in arguments that having boys on a team would hurt girls' athletic opportunities was the unarticulated assumption of male athletic superiority. No one ever argued that having a girl on a football team would take playing time away from a boy or that once a girl wrestled at the 103-pound level other schools would need to recruit girls in order to compete. People seemed to assume that one single boy could dominate a field hockey team and even a league. The director of the NJSIAA [New Jersey State Interscholastic Athletic Association], for example, argued in 1987 that having boys play on occasion would be unfair to other teams, because he assumed the coed team would be better than the all-female squad.

Further, pitting boys against girls would only emphasize the difference between the two. A 1991 editorial in the *St. Louis Post-Dispatch* argued that the size differential and physical athleticism of boys would overwhelm girls. The author quoted a college women's basketball coach ("within their context, girls' sports can be just as exciting, as dramatic, as anything as boys' sports") and reemphasized the words "within their context." Readers were reminded that [tennis champion] Chris Evert admitted she could not beat her brother, who did not play professional tennis. The editorial exemplified the assumption that males are essentially better athletes and that having coed teams would underline girls' athletic limitations. . . . By accentuating the need for separate boys and girls sports, especially in field hockey, these stories highlighted the public perception that girls, try as they might, could not really be competitive with boys.

Whether boys are inherently better field hockey players is mostly a matter of opinion, as indicated by the mixed results of coed field hockey teams. Sometimes female teams have been unable to defeat male teams. The 1998 undefeated Simsbury, Connecticut, High School girls' varsity team, for example, could not beat the fourteen boys against whom they practiced. The assumption of athletic superiority, however, has often been based solely on physical attributes, ignoring the role of skill in the game. One male sophomore who played in Massachusetts was described by his coach as faster and stronger than most of his teammates, but the coach added that the boy lacked stick-handling skills. He was not the best player on the team, but the coach admitted that he was an "impact" player. Further, despite presumed superior size, speed, strength, and aggressive qualities, usually one boy cannot dominate a team or a league. Many coaches who have boys on their squads have emphasized that they are often not the best on the team. After John Williams initially won the right to play in Pennsylvania, his team compiled a 4-11-4 record, indicating that one boy could not carry a field hockey team to a state title. Often boys would not make the varsity squad if allowed to play. Two in Maryland, denied the opportunity to play by the school district, were allowed to practice with the team and serve as its managers. The coach said that even had the district allowed them to play they were unlikely to make the squad as anything but practice players because one boy lacked stick-handling skills and the other was the slowest person on the field. . . .

Boys and Girls Should Be Allowed to Play on the Same Team

Ideologically, the issue of boys on girls' field hockey teams has been problematic. On the one hand, the feminist argument concerning traditionally male contact sports was clear and simple: Gender equality demanded that girls have a chance to play, and the equal protection clause and the equal rights amendments guaranteed that right. On the other hand, if the goal was to increase female participation and simultaneously promote gender equality, then the presence of boys in field hockey was a complicating factor. Although promoting and protecting girls' athletic programs was a strong pro-female position, the reasons for excluding boys from field hockey were often based on the same overbroad paternalistic generalizations that had been used to exclude girls from contact sports. People argued obliquely that boys are superior athletes because they are bigger, stronger, and faster than girls. Girls would be injured playing coed field hockey, boys would intimidate them, and then girls would quit the sport.

A Boy Playing on a Girls' Volleyball Team

Why would a boy want to play on a girls' volleyball team? A girl trying to play a boys' sport is seen by many as heroic, someone making a valiant effort in a sport. But a guy in a girls' sport is seen by many [as] him being a sissy. . . .

[Pete] Pezzella said he went out for the girls' team [at New Brighton High School, near Pittsburgh, Pennsylvania] because he loves volleyball. Although New Brighton has a club team for boys, he said it's not taken seriously. "Plus, I'm friends with about 95 percent of the girls on the team. They knew I wanted to play and they have accepted me."

Mike White,
"Trading Places/Boys Give Girls' Teams a Try,"
Pittsburgh Post-Gazette, *September 23, 2005.*

Although there may have been a certain practical reality to that argument, philosophically it was inconsistent with everything proponents of female participation in contact sports had argued because it accepted that girls are weak, frail, awkward, and timid athletes who need protection. It accepted the stereotype that boys, as a class, are better athletes than girls. In fact, by excluding all boys from girls' teams it might have promoted that very theory. One court warned that the stereotype might undermine the goal of promoting athletics for females. In 1979 the Massachusetts Supreme Court, ordering that boys not be excluded from girls' teams if no comparable team existed, wrote that "to immunize girls' teams totally from any possible contact with boys might well perpetuate a psychology of 'romantic paternalism' inconsistent with such development [of competitive athletics for girls] and hurtful to it in the long run."

Even if boys are in general better athletes after puberty, excluding them from field hockey to protect girls and their egos is an extreme reaction. The Massachusetts Supreme Court suggested that if girls were in such danger from large boys, then perhaps standards should be adopted limiting participants to a certain size and weight, regardless of gender, to avoid an overbroad generalization that all boys are bigger, stronger, and better athletes than all girls. If excluding girls' from boys' sports to save boys' egos is unacceptable, then so is the converse. Perhaps playing with boys would make girls better athletes, or perhaps it would teach them that they can compete with boys without undue risk of injury or embarrassment. . . .

What Field Hockey Players Think

In many ways the battle over field hockey, for youngsters who played and those who wanted to play, was the same as the struggle over other contact sports. Female players were not usually the ones who wanted to keep the sport female. Much like the boys on wrestling teams, girls were not overly upset at the notion of competing with boys. Twelfth-grade girls in Annapolis, Maryland, for example, believed that two boys who wanted to try out deserved a chance, and they said they would not be intimidated playing against boys. The girls' greatest concern was that boys would receive special treatment because they had less experience playing field hockey. Ten years later, girls on another Maryland team still supported the rights of two boys to try out for the squad and, using modern parlance, called for "gender equity." After having multiple teams forfeit to her coed field hockey team rather than play a team that had a male member, the female captain of the Chatham, Massachusetts, high school team said, "It just seems like the adults are getting in the way of our fun."

> *"Athletes are not just perceived as foot-ball players or cheerleaders. Instead they are perceived as male and female football players or cheerleaders."*

Athletes Are Judged According to Gendered Sports Stereotypes

Lisa A. Harrison and Amanda B. Lynch

Lisa A. Harrison is a professor at California State University, Sacramento. Her research interests are in social psychology, particularly stereotypes and the psychology of women. Psychology department graduate student Amanda B. Lynch assisted with the research in the following selection. Harrison and Lynch analyze research about how people perceive athletes based on the athletes' assumed thoughts and behaviors and the level of gender identification of three sports: football, basketball, and cheerleading. Athletes in sports that "matched" their gender were judged differently than those that "defied" their gender, although in unexpected ways.

Lisa A. Harrison and Amanda B. Lynch, "Social Role Theory and the Perceived Gender Role Orientation of Athletes," *Sex Roles: A Journal of Research*, vol. 52, February 2005, pp. 228–231, 235. Copyright © 2005 Springer. Part of Springer Science+Business Media. Reproduced with kind permission from Springer Science and Business Media and the authors.

As you read, consider the following questions:

1. What particular aspect of sport and the perceptions of an athlete's gender role are the authors investigating?

2. What was the gender role perception of boys and girls playing in gender-nontraditional sports, according to the authors?

3. What assumptions do the authors find to be made about the motivation of athletes playing gender-traditional sports?

It is not surprising to find that as early as grade one, stereotypes concerning the gender-appropriateness of athletics influence perceptions of and participation in athletic activities. A longitudinal study of kindergarten, first, and third graders demonstrated that young boys are more likely than young girls to believe they are good at sports, that it is important to do well in sports, and that sports are a constructive activity. Furthermore, boys are more likely than girls to enjoy sports. Subsequent research provides evidence that these gender differences persist over time. For example, [one researcher] studied male and female high school students and investigated whether individual students preferred to be remembered as an athletic star, a brilliant student, the most popular student, or as a school leader. They found that boys were more likely to wish to be remembered as an athletic star, whereas girls were more likely to wish to be remembered as a school leader. Only 9% of the girls, in comparison to the 36% of boys, wished to be remembered as an athletic star. Similarly, [another study] found that although most sports-related college activities were likely to be perceived as masculine, or both masculine and feminine, fewer women than men intended to participate in sport-related activities that were classified as masculine.

Perceived Masculinity and Femininity

Research on athletes' self-perceived gender role orientation suggests that there is a relationship among athletic participation and perceived masculinity and femininity. An earlier study showed that female athletes perceived themselves as lower in femininity, but not higher in masculinity, than their college peers. However, results of a more recent study ... suggest that students who participate in and identify with sports are more likely to have a masculine or androgynous gender role orientation, whereas students who do not participate or identify with sports are more likely to have a feminine gender role orientation. Yet, there is evidence that female athletes often experience significant conflict with the negotiation of their identities as both athletes and women. For example, a focus group study found that female athletes had difficulties reconciling their big, muscular, fit bodies with the small feminine body that is usually considered to be culturally ideal. Likewise, they were bothered that they differed from "normal girls" in terms of looks, clothing, social attention, and dating. However, they simultaneously expressed pride in their strong, fit bodies and their athletic abilities. These female athletes struggled to maintain a feminine identity that often clashed with stereotypical masculine characteristics such as competitiveness and aggression that made them successful in their sport. Thus, it is apparent that sports participation influences athletes' self-perceived gender role orientations, and female athletes often struggle to reconcile their identity as women and athletes. Likewise, there is evidence that athletic participation influences how others perceive the gender role orientation of female athletes. ...

Athletic participation also influences others' perception of athletes' gender role orientation and very often, athleticism is equated with masculinity. For example, [one study] examined college students' perceptions of athletes and found that female athletes were perceived as having both masculine (i.e., active and aggressive) and feminine characteristics (i.e., tactful and sensitive), but male athletes were only perceived as having masculine characteristics. Likewise, when [other researchers] surveyed a community sample in Iowa they found that participation in sports such as basketball, gymnastics, tennis, and track did not enhance or detract from the perceived feminine qualities of female athletes. However, this might have occurred because gymnastics is often perceived as feminine and basketball and tennis as gender-neutral. This may also be explained by a more recent study that showed that femininity and athleticism are generally perceived to be different constructs. Because female athletes are perceived as playing different roles on and off the athletic field, perceptions concerning the femininity of female athletes are more likely to be influenced by their behavior when they are not playing sports than their behavior when they are playing sports. Thus, athleticism may increase perceptions of masculinity in female athletes without directly reducing their perceived femininity.

Taken together, the studies described above suggest that the perceived gender role orientation of female athletes is related to their athletic role (although the nature of this relationship may be unclear). However, most researchers have neglected to determine if perceptions of gender role orientation are influenced by whether athletes participate in sports that are stereotypically feminine or masculine. Perhaps some of the conflicting findings from the above research are related to stereotypes and judgments concerning participation in different types of sports. In the present research we examined whether perceptions of athletes' gender role orientation are influenced by athletes' participation in stereotypically feminine or masculine sports.

Athletes Are Judged by the Gender of Their Sport

In the present study, we examined whether social role theory can explain the perceived gender role orientations of male and

female athletes who participate in either stereotypically feminine or masculine sports. Participants read an article that described a male or female athlete who was a football player, a
basketball player, or a cheerleader. Next, they completed the
Bem Sex Role Inventory (BSRI) to evaluate the perceived masculine gender role orientation (i.e., agency) and feminine gender role orientation (i.e., communality) of the athlete. In addition, participants rated their approval of the athlete and
indicated whether they believed the athlete's motivation to
participate in his/her sport was due to internal factors or external factors. According to social role theory, because specific
social roles are typically constraining, they should have an important influence on the perceptions of the athletes. Therefore, athlete gender should be less influential than the athletic
role fulfilled by the athlete. . . .

Participants read one of six newspaper articles that presented an interview with a high school athlete who had successfully competed in an athletic event. The articles varied the
athlete's gender and the sport played. One version of the article is below.

"Victory for Local High School"

An incredible day for sports fans ended with an exciting local victory last weekend when Jake, a football player for
Dayton High School, gave a winning performance in the last
few moments of the competition. Jake's outstanding performance did not go unnoticed as his coach, classmates, and
family shouted with delight when it was announced Dayton
High School's football team was the winner.

Jake has been a part of Dayton's football team for the last 3
years and will continue to participate next year for the varsity High School team. In his words, "Football is my life. . . .
I get out there every day with the hopes of becoming the
best football player ever." Practicing an average of 25 hr a
week, Jake has been working on that dream since an early

"Girl Wrestlers" Are Treated Differently Than "Wrestlers"

Before a match, when Lauren Clark-Johnson is silently preparing for her opponent, she can blend into a gym full of boys at a high school wrestling meet.

As a competitor in the 112-pound weight class, she has a wiry physique typical for a high school wrestler.

Once a match begins, Clark-Johnson, one of the best girl wrestlers in the state, no longer blends in with the boys. She often beats them. . . .

But Clark-Johnson and her colleagues are still learning how to deal with the negative, often painful fallout from beating boys at their own game. Girls aren't always given respect for winning and sometimes face resentment. Boys who lose to girls can face ridicule from teammates, parents and coaches. . . .

Javier Serna, "Girls Take Male Wrestlers to the Mat,"
News & Observer, January 11, 2009.

age and has been diligently focused on football for years. Anticipate more thrills next week when Dayton High School's football team competes at the finals!. . .

The Gender of the Sport Trumps the Gender of the Athlete

Based upon social role theory, it was predicted that athletic roles, rather than athlete gender, would primarily guide perceptions of athletes' gender role orientations. Overall, our research consistently supports this notion, inasmuch as we found that athlete gender did not significantly affect global perceptions of gender role orientation. However, we did find that athletic roles were important inasmuch as athletes who fulfill stereotypically masculine athletic roles (i.e., football and basketball) are likely to be perceived as having a masculine gender role orientation. Likewise, athletes who fulfill a stereotypically feminine athletic role (cheerleading) are likely to be perceived as having a feminine gender role orientation. Thus, our data suggest that the perceived gender role orientations of athletes are more likely to be affected by the athletic roles they fulfill than their gender. This research expands upon previous research that found people who fulfill traditional masculine social roles are more likely to be perceived as having masculine gender role orientations, whereas people who fulfill traditional feminine social roles are more likely to be perceived as having feminine gender role orientations.

We also predicted that athletic role and athlete sex would have a mutual influence upon the perceived gender role orientations of athletes. Specifically, we expected that the type of sport played would influence the perceived agency of female athletes, but not of male athletes. Conversely, we expected that type of sport participation would influence the perceived communality of male athletes, but not of female athletes. Our data support our hypotheses inasmuch as we found that female football players and basketball players were perceived as higher in agency than female cheerleaders, but type of sport did not influence the perceived agency of male athletes. Likewise, male cheerleaders were perceived as higher in communality than male football players and male basketball players, but type of sport did not influence the perceived communality of female athletes. Once again, our findings are consistent with the basic notions of social role theory. Although social roles, such as athletic role, have a powerful influence upon the perceived gender role orientation of athletes, this does not negate the influence of gender roles. Thus, athletes are not just perceived as football players or cheerleaders. Instead they are perceived as male and female football players or cheerleaders. Therefore, it appears that participation in gender nontraditional sports does not actually detract from the perceived femininity of female athletes and the perceived masculinity of male athletes. Instead, boys and girls who participate in gender nontraditional sports are likely to be perceived as having a more complex gender role orientation that consists of traditional masculine and feminine characteristics.

We also expected to find higher approval ratings for athletes who participate in gender traditional sports than for their counterparts who participate in gender nontraditional sports. However, our findings did not support this notion. Approval ratings for male athletes were equivalent, regardless of their athletic role. Conversely, there was lower approval of female athletes who participate in a gender traditional sport than of female athletes who participate in a gender nontraditional sport. It is unclear why the approval ratings for cheerleaders were so low. Previous research with adolescents suggests that girls' participation in cheerleading is associated with increased popularity and status, although this is moderated by resentment toward popular girls. Likewise, research suggests that cheerleaders are accorded a high level of prestige among high school students. Based upon our pilot study we deliberately chose this sport because of its overwhelming association with femininity. In addition, most high school cheerleading squads demand a high level of athleticism and competitiveness, which are also integral to most other sports. However, it has been argued that cheerleading is often not perceived to be a sport in the same manner as activities such as basketball and soccer. Thus, it is possible that although cheerleading is a popular activity that lends status to its participants, it is simultaneously devalued as not being a true sport. Previous research suggests that sports such as gymnastics, synchronized swimming, and figure skating are also perceived to be stereotypically feminine. It would be useful to investigate whether similar findings can be replicated with these traditionally feminine sports.

Assumptions About Athletes' Motivations

Our last prediction was that motivation attributions would be influenced by athletic roles. Internal attributions were expected to be made concerning the motivations of athletes that participate in gender nontraditional sports, whereas external attributions were expected to be made concerning the motivation of athletes who participate in gender traditional sports. We found some support for this notion. Specifically we found that male football players and female cheerleaders were perceived to be motivated by pressure from friends or family. Accordingly, it is feasible that many people believe that many athletes participate in gender traditional rather than gender nontraditional sports in order to achieve social approval from friends and family. In addition, we found that male football players were perceived to be motivated by financial reward, a finding that is understandable inasmuch as professional football players receive extremely high incomes. Thus, people may attribute athletes' participation in gender traditional sports as due to external factors because there are specific external factors (e.g., social approval, financial reward) that may result from participation in gender traditional sports. Conversely, we found that male cheerleaders and female football players were perceived to be motivated by a love for the sport. It may be that there is an intuitive understanding that male cheerleaders and female football players violate injunctive social norms concerning sport participation which could lead to social disapproval from others. In addition, it is unlikely that male cheerleaders or female football players receive significant financial reward for participation in their sport. Therefore, people may attribute athletes' participation in gender nontraditional sport as due to some internal factor, such as a love for the sport, because there appears to be few external motivations for participation in such sports.

Social role theory suggests that perceived gender role orientations are primarily dependent upon the social roles we fulfill. Previous research has shown that social roles related to sex-typed divisions of labor, both inside and outside the home, have a strong influence upon perceived gender role orientations. Thus, people who fulfill stereotypically feminine roles are more likely to be perceived as having feminine gender role orientations. Likewise, people who fulfill stereotypically masculine roles are more likely to be perceived as having masculine gender role orientations. The present research expands our understanding of social role theory by demonstrating that athletic social roles also influence perceptions of athletes' gender role orientations.

> *"Girls gravitated toward skateboarding and other forms of alternative youth culture as a way of off-setting the oppressive rules girls felt they 'had' to follow in order to be perceived as a certain kind of (popular) girl."*

Female Athletes Defy Gendered Sports Stereotypes

Deirdre M. Kelly, Shauna Pomerantz, and Dawn H. Currie

Deirdre M. Kelley is a professor of the sociology of education and Dawn H. Currie is a professor of sociology at the University of British Columbia in Vancouver. Shauna Pomerantz is an assistant professor in the department of child and youth studies at Brock University in Ontario. The following viewpoint is excerpted from their article, "'You Can Break So Many More Rules,'" which appeared in the book, Youth Culture and Sport. *The authors interviewed skateboarding girls about how they define themselves against skateboarding boys' and mainstream girls' culture. The authors found the girls often see themselves as leading alternative lifestyles not only because it is important to be different from the popular masses, but also because they enjoy skateboarding as a unique sport.*

As you read, consider the following questions:

1. How do the skateboarding girls interviewed by the authors explain the dearth of girls who skateboard?

2. According to the authors, what criticisms did the skateboarding girls make of the style and dress of the "bun girls"?

3. How did the "Park Gang Boycott" affect the behavior and perception of girls, according to the authors?

The "non-traditional" sport of skateboarding has a rich and vibrant history, dating back to its original incarnation in 1970s Californian surf culture. In the new millennium, many elements of the culture remain the same—a dedication to risk-taking, an affinity with punk rock (now splintered into pop punk, old school punk, hardcore, grindcore, and Goth) and more recently hip-hop, a love of baggy clothes, an interest in marijuana and "partying", a slacker reputation (think Bart Simpson from *The Simpsons*), and an anti-mainstream attitude. Given these defining features, it is interesting to note that corporate America has taken up skateboarding as one of its favorite marketing themes. Sports-oriented corporations, such as Nike and adidas, have worked hard to brand their products with skater "authenticity" in order to tap into the "cool" identity that many skaters cultivate. In response to this corporate branding, many skaters have opted to engage in fringe activities and cultural practices, including shopping at non-mainstream stores, participating in community-sponsored skate jams or competitions, reading on-line independent skater zines, and listening to "indie" or independent music.

Yet for all of skater culture's association with nonconformity and anti-mainstream values, it has been oddly traditional in its membership, dominated by boys and men. Boys have been the actors; girls the watchers, admirers, and supporters. It has also been overtly sexist from its inception. Skater girls regularly confront sexist assumptions about girls being unable to skate or as not having what it takes to be an "authentic" skateboarder. Skater girls are ignored, accused of merely wanting to boy-watch, insulted, and otherwise made to feel like outsiders in male-dominated skate parks. These sexist practices are corroborated in [Becky] Beal's ethnographic study of a group of young male skateboarders in Colorado. Beal found that while the boys created an alternative, or more cooperative masculinity, it was still defined by "differentiating and elevating themselves from females and femininity," thus maintaining "the privilege of masculinity."

Possibly as a result, girls have generally not taken up skateboarding in numbers large enough to count—making girls who decide to become skaters risk takers and rule breakers in more ways than one. . . . To be a girl skater is to resist . . . "emphasized femininity." In our interviews with skater girls in Vancouver, Canada, we found that girls gravitated toward skateboarding and other forms of alternative youth culture as a way of off-setting the oppressive rules girls felt they "had" to follow in order to be perceived as a certain kind of (popular) girl. Fourteen-year-old Sara explained that being a girl entails following "many" unspoken "rules"—rules which she felt were unfair and unnecessary: "That's why I like being alternative, because you can break so many more rules. If you hang out with the cliques and the mainstreamers and the pop kids, there's so many more rules that you have to follow. And if you don't follow [them] . . . you're no longer cool. . . ."

Skateboarding Girls Defy Their Alleged Limitations

In the minds of working-class skater girls like Grenn, to call skateboarding a "sport" seemed to associate it with the much-hated preps, who traditionally have used organized athletics, cheerleading, and dance squad as routes to social status within many North American schools. Regardless of this distinction, skateboarding requires physical strength, balance, agility, and bravery. To skate is to know how to fall and how to attempt complicated and risky tricks. Even the most basic trick, the ollie—where a skater smacks down the end of her board, moves her foot forward to bring the board up into the air, then lands smoothly with her feet equally apart in the middle of the board—runs the risk of injury.

Ollies, kickflips, grinding, and carving are all skater tricks that must be performed with the full knowledge that falling is likely, especially for beginners. "First, you've got to get the balance," explained Tori. "And then you've got to be fearless, because 24/7 . . . you're riding along cement. When you fall, it hurts. It doesn't just hurt a little bit—it hurts a lot. But in order to learn these tricks, you fall down a lot."

This kind of physical audacity is not generally associated with being a girl. As [one researcher] suggests, typical motility and spatiality for girls can be timid, uncertain, and hesitant, as many girls are not brought up to have the same kind of confidence and freedom in their movements as boys. [The researcher] sees femininity as based on a particular bodily comportment that is restrictive of large movements and risk-taking. Girls are not often seen to be capable of achieving physical acts that require strength and power or handling the pain that such physical acts can incur. Willingly inviting pain is seen to be boys' territory. Boys are ascribed the kind of confidence and craziness needed to carry skater tricks through to completion. Girls are not.

Skater girls in our study were aware of this gendered notion of motility and bodily comportment. When asked why girls did not skate as much as boys, [one skater girl] Onyx noted that girls might see skateboarding as "a guy thing to do. It is our thing to sit around and chit chat and gossip and stuff and watch them skateboard." Grover added, "Yeah, and some girls are kind of, like, scared." But Onyx retorted that she and her friends did not "think like that. We wanted to try it." Emily, too, reasoned that girls "don't want to continuously fall," and realized that skater boys are much less worried: "Like, guys there, they fall and they keep falling, but it's amazing, they always get back up and, like, try the same thing again."

Some Girls Set Themselves Apart with Practice

By "doing" skateboarding, girl skaters engaged in a transgressive bodily comportment. They were willing to stand with a wide gait on their boards, dangle their arms freely by their sides, and spread out for balance. They knowingly made spectacles out of themselves, courting the gaze of the skater boys and other onlookers. While some beginners were not keen to wipe out, others reported being less afraid. Pete enjoyed the adrenaline "rush," and Zoey added, "The first time I wiped out, I was just, like, 'Whoa!' I fell really hard. I was, like, 'Aahh!' kind of. And then I just wanted to do it again, because it was like, 'Wow!'" Despite a major "face plant" the first time she skateboarded, Kate recalled telling a "freaked out" friend: "I'm back on there still doing like weird stuff." Like Kate, Lexi evinced stoicism about her inevitable injuries: "I'm not very good, but if I get scraped, I'm not going to whine and bitch about it. I'm just going to go, 'Oh, damn. Okay.'" Tori and Priscilla, visibly scraped and bruised at the time of their interview, saw "road rash" as a badge of honor. The skater girls' toughness and relative lack of concern about bruises, scrapes, and scars provide a sharp contrast with dominant images of femininity.

No doubt part of the rush some of skater girls felt came from knowing they were engaged in an activity that most girls (and boys) did not have the guts to try. As Amanda suggested, most boys at the skate park were more "risk taking" than girls. "They don't care if they, like, get bruises and stuff. They'll be, like, 'Yeah! Cuts!' And then girls will be, like, 'Oh no!'" But some skater girls willingly accepted the risks involved in skateboarding as a way of setting themselves apart from emphasized femininity. Such work entailed dedication on the part of girls who wanted to be identified as skaters. The constant practice that goes along with mastering even the most basic trick (let alone learning how to stabilize yourself on the board, whether in motion or not!) separated the serious skater girls from those who mostly enjoyed being associated with the culture.

But as the comments from the girls suggest, there was a great deal of play in this hard work. Girls who skated displayed pride in their skills and were delighted to regale us with their "war stories." During their interview, Tori and Priscilla could hardly contain their enthusiasm for skateboarding and continuously jumped up from their seats to show scars and ollie-tears in their sneakers or to demonstrate how they balance on their boards. Lexi and Grenn, as well, displayed delight in being able to talk about skateboarding in their interview, and gleefully stood up to highlight their stances. The hard work that these girls put into skateboarding gave them bragging rights, endless amounts of fun, and a feeling of pride at being able to enter the male-dominated skater world. To the girls we spoke with, such pleasure was well worth the work. . . .

Skater Girls Embody an Alternative Identity

Equally important to defining their alternative identities was the skater girls' rejection of styles favored by a certain type of popular girl: tight, expensive designer jeans or skirts, "really tight tank tops," and lots of makeup. As Zoey explained, "A lot of the skater clothes aren't slutty, so that's really cool. . . . That really tight stuff—those can get really annoying after awhile, and you can't do *anything* on a board in it." According to Grover, "bun girls" (her group's name for the sexy-dressing popular girls at her school, all of whom regularly wore buns in their hair) wear "tanks tops four seasons a year.... They base a lot upon their looks and what they think the guys will like." "They're not really their own person," added Onyx. As Zoey declared, her skater friendship group was "totally the opposite" of girls who dress "sexy" to "attract guys," and her co-interviewee, Pete, agreed: "Dressing sexy kind of, in my perspective, attracts the wrong type of guys for me. I'm not into those guys ... that are attracted to sex appeal only [and not the brain]."

Forging an alternative identity through style was difficult work and often entailed defending one's choices against the mainstream trends. It also meant risking teasing from popular girls and the possibility of not being perceived as "dateable" by boys, some of whom were said to value overtly sexual style over an anti-mainstream, somewhat androgynous look. Grover liked a skater boy, for example, but noticed that his current girlfriend dressed in a traditionally feminine way. If "that's the type he likes," she noted matter-of-factly, "I wouldn't try to become a [sexy-dressing] bun girl just to satisfy him." The skater girls in our study were mainly interested in having boyfriends but felt that such pursuits needed to be conducted on their own terms and with as little attention to emphasized femininity as possible. Nevertheless, this identity work also elicited a great deal of play from the girls, many of whom took pride in scouring second-hand markets and pushing the boundaries of their own well-defined looks. As well, sometimes the cultivation of an alternative style fostered other playful features of identity, such as the creation of neologisms [new words], being in the know about certain kinds of music and films, and other elements of style, such as piercing, hair dying, and deck [skateboard] decoration. The work of forging an alternative femininity through style was rewarded by the enjoyment that embodying a creative and fun femininity brought to the girls.

Girls Aren't Always Welcomed by Skater Boys

The following story exemplifies the political struggle and intense work that some girls endure *en route* to becoming a skater and the pride and pleasure that can come from performing an alternative identity that has been hard won. The "Park Gang" is the name we have given to a group of eight skater girls, all friends or acquaintances who hung out at one skate park in Vancouver.

When members of the Park Gang decided to try skateboarding, they ventured into the skate park with their boards, hoping to gain acceptance and practice. The skate park they selected was considered amateurish compared to the larger and more daunting parks downtown. It was connected to a community center in an affluent neighbourhood and was relatively clean and safe. But the park proved to be a location of struggle, dominated as it was by skater boys who gave the girls a hard time. The boys were always asking members of the Park Gang to show them what they could do and constantly questioning the girls' abilities. The boys often asked Zoey, "Why don't you skate more?" She admitted that, "sometimes we don't want to skate around them 'cause, like, they do really good stuff and we're just kind of learning."

The Park Gang quickly realized that being the only girl skaters at the park singled them out for some harassment. To the skater boys who dominated the park and acted as its gatekeepers, the park was their space—a space that left very little room for girls, unless they were watchers, fans, or girlfriends. Gracie theorized that girls skate less than boys due to this kind of territorial attitude: "some [girls] are kind of, like, scared, because of what people might think of them." When asked what she meant, Gracie noted that the lack of girls who skated at the park might make the boys question girls' right to belong. Onyx added that the skater boys viewed the Park Gang as "invading their space." Grover felt that the Park Gang threatened the skater boys "just because, you know, girls are doing *their* sport."

This struggle eventually created tension for the Park Gang. Grover, Gracie, and Onyx understood that the boys were threatened by their presence but wished the boys could appreciate how hard it was for girls to get started. They wanted the boys to see them as equals who deserved the same kind of camaraderie that they showed each other. But instead, the boys saw them as interlopers with no legitimate claim to the space. Some of the boys accused some of the Park Gang of being posers. A poser wears the "right" clothes but does not really skate. Although boys can also be posers, girls who attempt access to skate parks are often singled out for this derogatory title. It is assumed that girls hang around the park as a way to meet skater boys.

Girls Prove Their Interest in the Sport

It was just such an accusation that prompted the Park Gang to take action collectively in order to prove the skater boys wrong. Zoey recounted the story.

> There's this one time where a couple of the guys thought we were just—they said it out loud that we're just there for the guys, and we're like, "No!" And they're like, "But you're here all the time, like almost every day, skateboarding, and so are we." So we did this whole thing where we didn't come there for quite awhile just to show [them]; and then we came back and they stopped bugging us about it.

The girls involved in the park boycott practiced away from the boys for two weeks. When asked what they had gained by boycotting the park, Zoey responded, "That we're not there just for the guys and we're not there to watch them and be

"I don't care if you did pitch a no-hitter! I still think you throw like a girl!" by Carroll Zahn, www.CartoonStock.com.

around them." Suddenly the girls received more respect and experienced less harassment from the skater boys. Zoey noted a distinct change in their attitude. "I guess to some level, they treated us like an equal to them, kind of." Instead of harassing the girls, the skater boys watched the Park Gang in order to see "how they were doing." They suddenly became curious about the girls' progress. When asked if they thought they had successfully changed the opinions of the skater boys, Zoey enthusiastically replied, "Well yes!"

The girls involved in the boycott retreated to a safe space where they were not being monitored and then re-emerged— triumphant. Through the boycott, the Park Gang challenged the skater boys' power and the ways in which girls are constructed through sexist and oppressive discourses. Before the boycott, the Park Gang were thought of in a very specific way: posers, flirts, and interlopers. After the boycott, the girls altered how the boys thought of them and, more significantly, how they thought of themselves. Through this political struggle, the Park Gang carved out a space for girls where none used to exist. In this way, the Park Gang engaged in the real work of changing how boys (and others) think about girls. But such hard work also legitimated their fun and opened the doors for other girls to use the park. As Pete pointed out, "lots of girls have actually started [skating] because my group started and then they kind of feel in power. I think they kind of feel empowered that they can start now, that it's okay for girls to skate."

> "Women's rugby operates with exactly the same set of rules as the men's game."

Women's Teams Play the Same Games as Men's Teams

Patricia Sanchez

Patricia Sanchez is a writer for City on a Hill Press, *a student-run newspaper at University of California, Santa Cruz (UCSC). At UCSC, rugby—men's and women's—is a club sport, which means the teams are not supported by the university's athletic department and do not fall under the jurisdiction of the National Collegiate Athletic Association (NCAA). In the following viewpoint, Sanchez describes the history and game of women's rugby at UCSC and highlights a few ways the women's game is different from the men's—even within the same rules and traditions.*

As you read, consider the following questions:

1. As Sanchez explains, how does women's rugby compare to women's basketball, lacrosse, and softball?

Patricia Sanchez, "Taking the Field, Fighting Stereotypes," *City on a Hill Press*, February 15, 2007. Reproduced by permission.

2. How does the author assert women's rugby has changed at UCSC since the days of inadequate resources and interest?

3. How did the women's rugby team finally secure funding from the school, according to Sanchez?

The UC [University of California] Santa Cruz [UCSC] women's rugby team is redefining the notion of "man's sport," one scrum at a time.

With broken bones, bloody noses and a few concussions, these girls give it their all despite the inherent dangers of such a violent game.

"We get hurt a lot," said Kathleen Daniel, a current player who suffered two concussions at her first tournament. "We already have like three players out and the season hasn't even started yet." After the tournament, Daniel agreed that she should have been taken out after the first concussion, but insisted at the time that it was no big deal.

The women on the team make it clear that they understand the fine line between playing injured and being hurt, because the sport requires a threshold and a tolerance for pain. But pain is just one of many things the women have to deal with. Especially in an aggressive sport like rugby, the team has to confront the stigmas that affect female athletes.

The physical nature of rugby leads many to assume that women who play the sport must either be especially masculine (or gay), or they must be playing an abridged version of the game—the team refutes both assumptions.

"Men in their older 20s, early 30s think there is something different about my sport," said Laurel Britton, a former UCSC rugger. "They think maybe we wear padding, or something, but we don't."

Rugby Is Rugby for Men or Women

Unlike basketball, where the regulation ball is slightly smaller for women; or softball, where the mound height, bat length and the number of innings are all different from baseball; or lacrosse, where the women's version of the game does not permit full contact—women's rugby operates with exactly the same set of rules as the men's game.

The women's team also follows with traditions like singing team songs and attending social gatherings with both teammates and opponents.

The team members take offense to the notion that women ought not to play what Scott Carson, the UCSC men's rugby head coach, described as traditionally "a ruffian's sport for gentlemen."

Kathleen Daniel expressed anger as she explained that she once had a male doctor tell her that it was inappropriate for a girl to play rugby.

"I don't feel he had a right to tell me that," Daniel said.

Laurel Britton also expressed dissatisfaction that the public is often shocked to see a woman playing a "man's sport."

"I talked to people on the plane [while flying to a playoff game last season] and I kind of got this sideways look when I told them I play rugby," Britton said.

Coach Carson recognizes that men often make unfair assumptions about women's rugby.

"[The women's game] has been called a gross bastardization of the sport," Carson said.

Sinan Dumlugo, a member of the men's rugby team, puts in some time helping out the women's team. He is hopeful that attitudes will soon change, but even he is of two minds about the women's game.

"[The game] is really not slower," Dumlugo said, discrediting the stereotype that women's sports are less exciting than men's. "You just have to look at it more patiently."

Another common stereotype that the women face is the idea that female athletes are ultra masculine. Female athletes are often judged on these grounds.

"People tend to think women players are dykes," Britton said.

Daniel, who is a lesbian, recalled signing up for the team with her girlfriend at the yearly OPERS [office of physical education, recreation, sporting, and wellness] festival and noticed that the rugby table was stationed right next to the Gay, Lesbian, Bisexual and Transgender (GLBT) table—though she was unsure as to whether that was intentional.

There does exist a gay-friendly organization called the International Gay Rugby Association and Board that promotes the sport to lesbians and gay men around the world, but for the most part the women's rugby team scoffed at the idea that the game inherently appealed to any sexual orientation.

Women's Interest in Sports Is on the Rise

Changing the negative perceptions about female athletes has and will continue to pose a challenge. However, support and equal opportunity for women in athletics has risen markedly over the past few decades.

Title IX, a law that passed in 1972, requires that women receive equal opportunities in public school sports. Rita Walker is UCSC's Title IX director, and makes sure that the school complies with the current expectations of the state in connection with the law.

Walker has personally seen the increase in opportunities for women in athletics. When Walker was in school in the '60s and '70s, elementary and middle school girls could only cheerlead because there were no women's sports teams, she said. Walker, who graduated high school one year after the law was passed, could not get enough support to start a women's basketball team just several years prior.

Turkish Soccer Is Not Just for Men

Soccer is now popular among women all over the world, and Turkish women, too, play "the beautiful game." As a matter of fact, there is a Turkish women's league, and many pundits in the business world think that women's soccer in this country is developing and attracting more and more fans.

"Some people come to watch a women's [league] game out of curiosity and with the prejudice that soccer is solely a male sport in the back of their minds," [said] Dr. Erden Or, the . . . women's soccer development officer. "But they become flabbergasted upon seeing the tough competition and the skills these girl display on the pitch and say, 'Bravo!' or, 'She can even play on our men's team!'"

Esra Maden,
"Turkish Women Play the Beautiful Game,"
Sunday's Zaman, *February 22, 2009.*

"My freshman year of high school, we organized into a basketball team scheduling our own practices and games with other schools," Walker said. "The only thing we needed was one teacher to ride with us and we could not get one teacher to agree."

Kevin "Skippy" Givens, the director of intramural and club sports at UCSC, has also seen the progression of women in sports during his lifetime.

"I have two younger sisters and when we were growing up they didn't have those opportunities," Givens said. "They were just as athletic as I was, but since they didn't have the opportunities they just laid dormant."

Support for the women's rugby teams has shown a significant improvement in the last 10 years at UCSC, as well.

"[In 2002] they didn't even have enough people to field 15 to a side, so they'd have to pick up players from the other team just to get a game played," Givens said. Givens claims that the women's rugby team was falling apart because the team's resources were no longer adequate and the sport was weakly advertised. A lack of funding and university recognition really hurt the team.

Britton recalled her time with the team last year [2006] when the women didn't even have uniforms to wear.

"We had to wear big, baggy, old men's jerseys because we didn't have any money," Britton said. "Students would have to buy their own equipment and sometimes we'd use hand-me-downs from the guys or old team members."

But like most of the setbacks the team has been dealt, Daniel said that the team found a way to brush it off.

"We don't care how we look," she said. "If we wanted to do that we'd play volleyball with those tight-ass shorts or something. We're playing to have fun."

Several years ago, in an attempt to fundraise, the rugby players created and tried to market team calendars featuring semi-nude photos of the players. But they received complaints that the calendar was anti-feminist and stopped selling it.

Permanent funding for the team was finally established last spring when students passed a referendum to provide club sports teams with university funding.

"It's $2,000 and it's really not much if you look at their overall budget," Givens said. "But it is something coming from the university and it certainly does help."

Reactions to the Sport

Though support from the university is on the rise, at times even the players' family members worry about their loved ones' involvement with such a violent sport.

After her son tore his PCL [posterior cruciate ligament in the knee] and underwent surgery as a result of a rugby injury, Terri McMahon, mother of team member Kelly McMahon, was apprehensive about seeing her daughter play.

"When [Kelly] told us she was playing rugby, we said, 'Oh my god, not again,'" Terri McMahon said. "But what could we do, tie her down with a ball and chain?"

Kelly's father, Michael McMahon, said that he enjoys watching women play because of the sportsmanship the team displays.

"It's not a single superstar or a single dunk; it has to be a team sport," he said. "They derive their strength from the team."

Sinan Dumlugo also appreciates women rugby players, though he seems to have different reasons.

"[They] remind me of that Foster's commercial of a girl that's gorgeous and then takes a beer can and crushes it on her head," Dumlugo said. "I would propose to her on the spot."

Mercedes Evangelista, a returning player, tries her best to live above the stereotypes that surround women in her sport; instead she just focuses on playing and having fun.

"I never thought of it as a male-only sport," Evangelista said. After all, "It's 2007."

> *"Girls gain confidence from facing what usually is stronger, faster, more athletic male competition."*

Girls' Teams Lack the Skill of Boys' Teams

Preston Williams

Preston Williams is a reporter for the Washington Post. *He writes the* Varsity Letter, *a weekly column about high school sports in the Washington, D.C., area. The following viewpoint is a response to a December 6, 2006, position statement by the National Collegiate Athletics Association (NCAA) Committee on Women's Athletics that discourages co-educational practice. Their argument was that it undermines the value of female athletes and violates the spirit of Title IX legislation promoting the gender equity of school athletic programs. The viewpoint author argues that at the high school level, co-ed practice benefits girls and boys.*

As you read, consider the following questions:

1. Why do coaches of girls' basketball teams occasionally pit their players against boys' basketball teams, according to Williams?

2. What is a secondary benefit that Williams identifies of having girls' teams practice with boys' teams?

3. As the author reports, how do co-ed practice games differ from regular games for both the girls and the boys?

An NCAA [National Collegiate Athletic Association] committee thinks it's a bad idea for women's basketball teams to practice against men. Its proposal is receiving the same kind of response from high school girls' basketball coaches that it got from NCAA women's basketball coaches:

"Huh?"

High school girls' basketball teams . . . , including many of the best, on occasion practice against boys' teams, usually the school's freshman or junior varsity squad. The girls' coaches believe that such encounters better prepare their players to face other formidable girls' programs.

The college-level discussions started with the NCAA Committee on Women's Athletics, which proposed limiting or banning the use of men in women's practices because it raises gender equity concerns and "is a threat to the growth in female participation at all levels." The proposal has no bearing on the high school game, but the debate does resonate in high school athletics, because it's very common for girls' teams to bring in boys for scrimmaging, particularly when the postseason draws near.

"I don't know what other options you have when you want to compete at the higher level," Oakton [Vienna, Va.] Coach Fred Priester said. "If the women can't be challenged, then how are they going to get better?"

Girls Improve by Playing Against Better Athletes

The girls gain confidence from facing what usually is stronger, faster, more athletic male competition. "If we can do it against them, we can most definitely do it against other girls," Edison [high school in Alexandria, Va.] All-Met guard Doreena Campbell said. Meantime, the boys often come away with a greater appreciation for the girls' game.

River Hill [Clarksville, Md.] senior forward-center Kelsey Erdman did not need validation from a boy last year [2006] to realize her team was formidable. They ended up 28-0 and winning the Maryland 3A championship. But when one boy said, "Wow, you guys are good!" after practicing against the Hawks, Erdman realized she and her teammates were gaining respect for themselves, and for their sport.

"They'd say things about Keisha Eaddy [now at Temple University in Philadelphia] and about how she was really good, and that our team was better than they thought," said Erdman, who also has practiced against boys in soccer and lacrosse. "It can help bring more [male] fans and people who appreciate the game more."

"When you have guys playing against girls," Notre Dame Academy [Middleburg, Va.] girls' coach Mike Teasley said, "and they see that they're physical and going to get up and down and run and can shoot and are fundamentally sound, it does create . . . respect."

Lee [Springfield, Va.] junior varsity [JV] boys' coach Vernon Lee, whose team in recent years has scrimmaged against the varsity girls, has noticed that when his players come back from away games, they cheer on the varsity girls in their home game, and the varsity girls cheer on the JV boys before boarding the bus for a road game.

"It seems now as though the kids are both rooting for both programs," Lee said. "They're supporting each other. They want each other to be successful."

Boys Are Directed to Play Easier Against Girls

Girls occasionally practicing against boys is an extension of summertime co-ed pick-up games, but it's a more controlled

Winning Times for the 2008 World Rowing Junior Championships (Under Age 19)

1,000 m Race	Women's Times (min:sec)	Men's Times (min:sec)	Difference in Times (sec)
One rower, sculling	04:09.97	03:37.75	−32.22
Two rowers, sculling	03:44.51	03:30.58	−13.98
Four rowers, sculling	03:28.45	03:05.89	−22.56
Two rowers, sweep	03:54.83	03:31.43	−23.40
Four rowers, sweep	03:34.97	03:10.78	−24.19
Eight rowers, sweep	03:13.03	02:58.04	−14.99

TAKEN FROM: Fédération Internationale des Sociétés d' Aviron (FISA), World Rowing Junior Championships in Ottensheim, Austria, 2008.

environment. The score is generally not kept and the boys are usually discouraged from making special efforts to block shots and make steals.

"I tell the guys before we start that this isn't about their ego, this is about them doing us a favor to help us get a little bit better," Priester said.

A lot of the work is situational—breaking a press, honing a press, executing a motion offense. Facing taller, quicker players with wider wingspans on a Thursday afternoon can really pay off on a Friday night, and the presence of the boys can spark a starting five that has grown weary of schooling its understudies.

"You find out that the boys don't want to lose to the girls," said Holy Cross girls' coach Russell Davis, whose Pallotti [Laurel, Md.] teams used to practice against the JV boys (Holy Cross is an all-girls school [in Kensington, Md.]). "The intensity level is a lot higher than what you could produce. It's almost like a game-type level of intensity."

Co-Ed Practice Improves the Whole Sport

Stonewall Jackson [Manassas, Va.] girls' coach Nsonji White has a regular boys' scout team made up of players not on the Raiders' school teams. As far as he's concerned, his scout team is a necessity.

"The reason is that last year I had six serious players and the rest filling a roster," White wrote in an e-mail. "I owed it to my program and those girls to challenge them. It aided in changing my girls' thinking. We won most of the scrimmages. What that has done to the confidence and attitudes of my girls has been tremendous."

Few area male coaches of girls' basketball teams have the perspective on the topic that Notre Dame's Teasley has. His sister is [Women's National Basketball Association] Washington Mystics guard Nikki Teasley, who grew up playing frequently against boys.

"Even though the women's game has grown a lot over the years, you can't match that when you're practicing with girls," Mike Teasley said. "It's no discredit to the women's game, or the women involved in the game. It's just about helping the game grow."

Periodical Bibliography

The following articles have been selected to supplement the diverse views presented in this chapter.

Johanna A. Adriaanse and Janice J. Crosswhite — "David or Mia? The Influence of Gender on Adolescent Girls' Choice of Sport Role Models," *Women's Studies International Forum*, September–October 2008.

Sean Cavanagh — "Sports in the City," *Education Week*, October 21, 2008.

Kelly E. Flanagan, et al. — "The Effect of Gender Opportunity in Sports on the Priorities and Aspirations of Young Athletes," *Sport Journal*, Spring 2006. www.thesportjournal.org.

Patrick W.C. Lau, Antoinette Lee, and Lynda Ransdell — "Parenting Style and Cultural Influences on Overweight Children's Attraction to Physical Activity," *Obesity*, September 2007.

Weidong Li, Amelia M. Lee, and Melinda A. Solmon — "Gender Differences in Beliefs About the Influence of Ability and Effort in Sport and Physical Activity," *Sex Roles: A Journal of Research*, January 2006.

Jill Painter — "Marta Could Give Fans a Reason to Watch Soccer," *San Gabriel Valley Tribune*, March 2, 2009.

Sandy Ringer — "Puyallup Wrestler Could Become First Girl State Champ" *Seattle Times*, February 16, 2006.

Dorothy L. Schmalz and Deborah L. Kerstetter — "Girlie Girls and Manly Men: Children's Stigma Consciousness of Gender in Sports and Physical Activities," *Journal of Leisure Research*, Fall 2006.

Jeffrey Thomas — "U.S. Gender-Equity Law Led to Boom in Female Sports Participation," U.S. Department of State's Bureau of International Information Programs, April 1, 2008. www.america.gov.

How Does Sports Participation Affect Girls' Health?

Chapter Preface

According to the Guttmacher Institute, a nonprofit organization focused on sexual and reproductive health research, policy analysis, and public education, in its 2006 report on U.S. teenage pregnancy statistics, 9.51 percent of teenage girls (from ages 15 to 19) became pregnant in 1972. According to the April 14, 2008, National Vital Statistics Report, that number had dropped to 7.22 percent by 2004. This rate decrease translates to approximately 200,000 fewer pregnancies each year. Also in 1972 came the passage of Title IX—which guaranteed girls equal access to education and sports resources—and the subsequent rise in girls' sports participation. The Web site of the National Association for Girls and Women in Sport calculates that fewer than 300,000 girls played high school sports in 1972; the National Collegiate Athletic Association (NCAA) counted more than 3,000,000 girls playing in 2007.

The drop in teen pregnancy is not generally attributed to the rise in girls' sports participation; obviously, many more cultural changes have occurred since 1972 than athletic demographics. Birth control advancements and sexual education campaigns are usually credited for the decline in pregnancy rates, followed by a correlation with a decrease in juvenile crime. When the health benefits of regular athletic activity are lauded by doctors and in the media, the topic is usually presented within the context of childhood obesity. When teen pregnancy is discussed as a health issue, it is usually within the context of the health of the baby or the financial cost of supporting young mothers. Any link between girls participating in sports and the reduced rate of teen pregnancy is made indirectly: girls who play sports are thought to have better self-esteem, and girls with better self-esteem are thought to make better choices about sex.

Recent research, however, suggests that there is a direct link between a girl's athletic involvement and her sexual health decisions. A 2004 article published by Stephanie Jacobs Lehman and Susan Silverberg Koerner in the *Journal of Youth and Adolescence*, "Adolescent Women's Sports Involvement and Sexual Behavior/Health," includes the results of a survey of high school girls. Girls involved in organized team sports take fewer sexual risks (such as combining sex with alcohol), demonstrate more positive sexual and reproductive health behaviors (such as seeking out or using birth control reliably), and have better sexual and reproductive health in general (such as fewer sexually transmitted diseases). When the participants of the study were asked to discuss their feelings about sports, they frequently stated that athletics had given them a sense of power and control over their lives and their bodies—control they did not relinquish in sexual situations. Aware of what their bodies were capable of and what they could do, these girl athletes took care of themselves by keeping their bodies healthy and fit so that their bodies would always be ready to serve them, in game play and in life.

Pregnancy is not a disease or injury, but it does have a physiological and psychological impact on a woman, especially on a young woman who has not finished her education and who may not have access to the financial and social resources available to older mothers. Pregnancy is especially limiting to an athlete, because it taxes her physical resources and dramatically changes the shape of her body and thus the way she moves and balances. She could hurt herself playing sports; she could hurt the fetus; she is not likely to be allowed by doctors or coaches to be a part of a team. There are options and social assistance for pregnant girls and young mothers who want to continue their education, but there are no solutions to the problem of pregnant athletes who still want to play.

The authors in the following chapter address other topics that relate girls' health to their participation in sports and compare the physical and psychological benefits of being athletic to some of the drawbacks of training and competing on organized teams.

| *"Sports offers unique protection against adolescent suicidality by providing social support and integration."*

Team Sports Are Associated with a Reduced Risk of Suicide in Girls

Lindsay A. Taliaferro, et al.

Lindsay Taliaferro is a doctoral candidate in the department of human health and behavior at the University of Florida at Gainesville; her co-authors are all professors in the departments of health and education at the same institution. Prior research found that increased rates of physical activity in girls indicated an increase of suicide risk, but the authors of this viewpoint reveal that solitary physical activity combined with dietary supplements and weight-loss attempts is different than participating in an athletic program with adult guidance and a strong, friendly support network of teammates. Sports, not exercise, reduce the risk of suicide for girls.

Lindsay A. Taliaferro, et al., "High School Youth and Suicide Risk: Exploring Protection Afforded Through Physical Activity and Sport Participation," *Journal of School Health*, vol. 78, October 2008, pp. 545–53. Copyright © 2008 American School Health Association. All rights reserved. Reproduced by permission of Blackwell Publishers.

As you read, consider the following questions:

1. What two behaviors do the authors identify are likely to be exhibited by girls who engage in some exercise each week?

2. What do the authors assert is the relationship between increased levels of exercise and suicidal behavior in males and in females?

3. What benefits, beyond improved physical health, does participating in a sport confer upon girls that reduce their risk of suicide, according to the authors?

Suicide represents the third leading cause of death for youth 15 to 24 years, accounting for 12.9% of all deaths in this age range. According to the Centers for Disease Control and Prevention (CDC), between 2003 and 2004, the suicide rate increased 18% for youth under age 20, and suicides constituted the only cause of death that increased among adolescents. In 2004, youth 15 to 24 years represented 14.2% of the US population and comprised 13.3% of the suicides. Though females attempt suicide more often than males, young males aged 15 to 19 are 3.6 times more likely than females to complete suicide. Further, for each completed suicide, an estimated 100 to 200 adolescents attempted to take their own lives. Thus, *Healthy People 2010* [a national health promotion and disease prevention initiative] specifically targets reducing the rate of completed suicide and the rate of attempted suicide among adolescents. The National Institute of Mental Health urges researchers to focus on decreasing the adolescent suicide rate by studying risk and protective factors.

Research indicates that physical activity affords the same psychological benefits to adolescents as to adults. Physical activity promotes positive emotional well-being including improvements in depressed mood, anxiety and stress, and self-esteem. Therefore, through its effect on psychological well-being, physical activity may protect against suicidality. Physical activity in the context of team sports may afford additional protection by facilitating social support and integration. Conversely, youth involved in sport may benefit from psychosocial advantages that increase the likelihood of participation. . . .

Physical activity, especially when combined with team sports, related to lower rates of suicidal behavior for males. Yet, frequent, vigorous aerobic activity, especially *without* team sports, related to higher rates of suicidal behavior for females. . . .

Results from the 2005 Youth Risk Behavior Survey

Of 13,857 adolescents, 16.9% had seriously considered attempting suicide, 13.3% had made a suicide plan, 9.0% had attempted suicide, and 4.2% had attempted suicide multiple times. Most (81.8%) had engaged in physical activity at least once per week, and 54.0% participated in sports. . . . Males were more likely than females to participate in physical activity at least once per week (87.1% vs 77.0%, respectively). Males also showed higher rates of sport participation than did females (61.0% vs 47.6%, respectively). Females demonstrated increased prevalence of suicidality, with 21.8% reporting thoughts or behavior, compared with 11.7% of males. . . .

After controlling for sport participation, we found no relationship between low or moderate levels of physical activity and suicidality among male adolescents. However, males who exercised 6 to 7 times/week showed reduced risk of planning suicide, attempting suicide, and attempting suicide multiple times. Conversely, females who exercised 1 to 2 times/week were more likely to feel hopeless, compared to inactive females. Though we did not find a significant difference in the rates of physical activity between females who reported suicidal behavior and those who did not, our findings revealed a link between suicidality and intention motivating exercise behavior. Specifically, females who exercised 1 to 2 or 6 to 7 times/week to lose weight demonstrated increased suicide risk. Furthermore, females who engaged in some physical activity each week were more likely to consume fewer calories or foods low in fat and to take diet supplements to lose weight. These 2 behaviors significantly increased suicide risk.

Sport participation was significantly associated with reduced odds of hopelessness and suicidal behavior among both genders. Male athletes were less likely to feel hopeless, and consider, plan, or attempt suicide. Highly involved male athletes had reduced odds of feeling hopeless and of considering or planning suicide than nonathletes. Female athletes demonstrated reduced risk of hopelessness, considering suicide, planning suicide, and attempting suicide multiple times. Compared to nonathletes, highly involved female athletes were less likely to feel hopeless or consider suicide. . . .

Results Are Consistent with Other Researchers'

Our findings also support relationships found by [J.] Unger and by [D.] Brown and [C.] Blanton. Unger, who determined the relative risk of suicidality associated with 6 physical activity/team sports combinations, found consistently lower rates of suicidal behavior among males who engaged in various levels of physical activity. However, female exercisers, especially those who performed high-intensity activity, demonstrated increased suicide risk. Though our study did not find as many statistically significant relationships between physical activity and suicidal behavior, the results for males and females generally support Unger's findings.

Similar to methods by Brown and Blanton, we controlled for sport participation in our physical activity analysis. Their study found that male college students who participated in low-intensity activity demonstrated reduced suicide risk. However, neither moderately nor vigorously active men showed

A Comparison of Sports Participation and Suicidality in Adolescents

Variable	Males		Females	
	n	%	n	%
Physical activity				
No physical activity	810	12.9	1590	23.0
1 to 2 times/week	1024	16.2	1603	23.2
3 to 5 times/week	2149	34.1	2396	34.7
6 to 7 times/week	2319	36.8	1313	19.0
Sport participation				
No sport	2444	39.0	3609	52.4
Sport participant	3818	61.0	3281	47.6
Level of sport involvement				
No sport	2444	39.0	3609	52.4
Moderately involved (1–2 teams)	2744	43.8	2664	38.7
Highly involved (3+ teams)	1074	17.2	617	9.0
Hopelessness and suicidal behavior				
Felt sad or hopeless	1417	21.5	2719	38.1
Thought about suicide	772	11.7	1558	21.8
Planned suicide	641	9.7	1187	16.6
Attempted suicide	371	6.3	745	11.5
Multiple suicide attempts	174	3.0	349	5.4

TAKEN FROM: Lindsay A. Taliaferro et al., "Table 1," "High School Youth and Suicide Risk: Exploring Protection Afforded Through Physical Activity and Sport Participation," *Journal of School Health* 78, no. 10, October 2008.

decreased risk in Brown and Blanton's study. Similar to findings by Unger, Brown and Blanton we found that physically active women demonstrated increased risk compared to less active women. . . .

Consistent with previous research, we did not find a significant difference in the rates of physical activity behavior between females who reported suicidal tendencies and those who did not. However, for females, exercising to lose weight, as well as restricting calories or taking diet supplements to attain the same goal, significantly increased suicide risk. Therefore, among females in our sample, findings regarding suicide risk and physical activity appear to support theories that suggest a complex relationship between body image and suicidal behavior.

Our findings indicate that physical activity alone may not protect against adolescent suicidality, especially among young females. Positive relationships between physical activity and reduced suicidality found in past research that used a composite independent variable may reflect the effects of sport rather than the benefits provided by physical activity.

The Particular Benefits of Sport Participation

Findings regarding sport participation support previous investigations that compared the relative risk of suicidal behavior between athletes and nonathletes. After controlling for physical activity, sport participation remained a significant factor in reducing suicidality among both genders. Compared to nonathletes, male athletes showed reduced risk of feeling hopeless and considering, planning, or attempting suicide. Young males involved in multiple sports attained even greater protection against hopelessness and suicidality than nonathletes. Compared to nonathletes, female athletes demonstrated reduced risk of hopelessness, considering suicide, planning suicide, and attempting suicide multiple times. Highly involved female athletes were less likely to feel hopeless or consider suicide than nonathletes. These findings support Brown and Blanton's investigation of sport's effect on suicidal behavior among college students.

Research suggests that physical activity provides significant mental health benefits. Our findings indicate that, in addition to physical activity, sport may protect against suicidality through other mechanisms. We hypothesize that sport offers unique protection against adolescent suicidality by providing social support and integration. Youth who report strong social support exhibit higher levels of resilience, less hopelessness, and reduced suicide risk. Adolescents demonstrate less suicide risk if they perceive family, friends, and peers as accepting; possess more positive friendships; and feel connected to school. [Researchers] found that the friendship environment affected suicidality for both males and females. However, for females, social network effects played an especially prominent role. Females who were socially isolated from the adolescent community demonstrated significantly greater suicide risk than females embedded in cohesive friendship groups.

Extracurricular activities provide adolescents an opportunity to establish positive social relationships and networks. [Another study] examined relationships among sport, other extracurricular activities, psychological factors, and suicidal behavior. Findings indicated that "those involved in team sports at school (alone or combined with other activities) . . . were most likely to report high self-esteem and were least likely to report sadness, anxiety, and suicidal behavior." These authors concluded that engaging in any organized activity imparted some benefit, but sport participation afforded unique positive advantages.

Athletes may experience greater social integration when they become members of a social network that includes teammates, coaches, health professionals, family, and community. The team sport environment represents a fertile ground for adolescent self-esteem development because teams provide opportunities for youth to engage with adults and peers to achieve collective goals. Through its capacity to foster feelings of social support and integration, sport participation may create a distinct form of protection against risk factors associated with adolescent suicide. Females, especially, may benefit from physical activity performed in the context of team sports. In addition to athletic competition, females also participate in sport to improve their fitness levels, improve their athletic skills, and enjoy group interaction. A report from The President's Council on Physical Fitness and Sports noted that "sport participation can enhance mental health by offering adolescent females positive feelings about body image, improved self-esteem, tangible experiences of competency and success, and increased self-confidence." Research supports the positive association between sport participation and improved self-concept among young females.

> "At lower levels of enjoyment, partaking in sporting activities may actually undermine self-esteem."

Sports Participation Does Not Always Enhance Girls' Self-Esteem

David R. Shaffer and Erin Wittes

David R. Shaffer is a professor emeritus of the psychology department at the University of Georgia at Athens. His research interests are in social and developmental psychology, particularly attitude change and self-concept/self-esteem development; Erin Wittes wrote the first draft of the following viewpoint as a master's thesis under the direction of Shaffer. Her research examines the idea that participating in sports before college enhances girls' self-esteem during college. The authors conclude it is actually a clear perception of sports' benefits that improves girls' self-esteem and sports participation may actually hurt girls who don't enjoy it.

David R. Shaffer and Erin Wittes, "Women's Precollege Sports Participation, Enjoyment of Sports, and Self-Esteem," *Sex Roles: A Journal of Research*, vol. 55, August 2006, pp. 225–32. Copyright © 2006 Springer. Part of Springer Science+Business Media. Reproduced with kind permission from Springer Science and Business Media and the authors.

As you read, consider the following questions:

1. What hypothesis did the authors make about the girls who enjoy sports the most?

2. What three contributors to sports enjoyment do the authors list that reliably predicted girls' sports enjoyment and self-esteem in college?

3. Why do the authors warn readers that the research sample of mostly white individuals could fail to predict sports enjoyment and self-esteem across racial or cultural lines?

Sports and sporting activities play a prominent role in many persons' lives. Millions of spectators passionately track the fortunes of their favorite teams and athletes, and a sizable number of sports enthusiasts participate in one or more athletic activities, either as formal participants in athletic competitions or for recreational purposes. What benefits do people derive from sporting activities, and to what extent does their own participation influence their sense of self?

Reasons for participating in sports are many and varied, including, but not limited to, enjoyment of the activity, peer and parental influence, presumed health benefits of participation, and an increase in physical conditioning/well-being. Among the most common presumed psychosocial benefits of sports participation is an enhanced sense of self-worth. Research on male samples is generally consistent with the latter assertion, which suggests that sports participation may have both short-term and long-term effects on persons' self-esteem.

Our focus in the present research centers on a presumed motivation for participating in sports and psychosocial benefits of such sports participation in young women. Several researchers have noted that sports and athletic activities are still generally considered to be a masculine domain and that girls may have difficulty reconciling the physical and competitive nature of sports with their emerging feminine self-concepts. Yet, girls' and women's participation in athletics has increased dramatically in the past 30 years, owing, in part, to the passage and enforcement of Title IX, a federal law passed in 1972 that bans discrimination on the basis of gender in federally funded institutions. Moreover, encouragement of girls to participate in sports is apparent in such popular cultural appeals as the late 1990s advertising campaign by Nike that featured young girls pleading "If you let me play sports" and then citing various health and psychosocial benefits that purportedly result from sport participation, including an enhanced sense of self-esteem.

Sports Participation Versus Sports Enjoyment

Previous research on the relationship between girls' sports participation and self-esteem is limited and somewhat inconsistent. Several researchers have reported bivariate relationships that indicate that girls (and boys in mixed-gender samples) who participate in sports have higher self-esteem than those who do not. Other researchers have reported that whether sports participation is positively or negatively related to participants' self-esteem is moderated by participants' gender role orientations and the nature of the sporting activity; for example, individuals with a feminine gender role orientation are most likely to derive a sense of self-worth from participating in noncompetitive than in competitive sports. Yet, it is worth noting that sports participation has been, at best, a modest predictor of global self-esteem for participants of either sex. . . .

Although sports participants of both sexes cite health benefits and social stimulation as reasons for participating in sports, the most frequently cited motive participants give is affective or evaluative in character. Sports are "fun," "exciting," or "activities that I enjoy." This finding suggests an interesting motivational model of girls' sports participation that, to our knowledge, has not been evaluated. Perhaps the positive relationship between girls' sport participation and self-esteem is mediated (or moderated) by the extent to which girls report that they enjoy sporting activities. Far fewer girls than boys regularly participate in sports, and their participation often stems from formal and informal inducements to participate from gym teachers, parents, siblings, or peers. We propose that girls who discover that they enjoy sporting activities during childhood or adolescence may experience gains in self-esteem from their participation, whereas those who derive little enjoyment from sports participation may benefit little from, or even suffer psychosocially from, continued involvement in activities they dislike or perhaps think of as stereotypically masculine endeavors. Indeed, [Sandra] Bem and [E.] Lenney found that partaking in behaviors perceived to be more appropriate for members of the other sex is often discomforting and produces negative feelings about the self. Thus, one goal of the present research was to evaluate the simple but straightforward mediating/moderating model ... that specifies that sports participation fosters the self-esteem of young women who report that they enjoy sporting activities and that, at lower levels of enjoyment, partaking in sporting activities may actually undermine self-esteem.

Of course, empirical support for the above hypotheses raises the issue of why girls might come to enjoy (or to derive little enjoyment from) sporting activities in the first place. We hypothesized that girls who come to enjoy sports the most are those who can point to clear benefits that they receive from their participation. Such benefits may be many and varied, although it is likely that sports-related enhancements to such personal attributes as physical competence, a favorable body image, and socially desirable masculine characteristics such as assertiveness and a healthy sense of competition, contribute heavily to girls' enjoyment of sports and to any enhanced sense of self-worth they may experience from their participation. A related corollary is that girls who fail to experience such benefits derive little if any enjoyment or enhanced self-worth from sporting activities. Our research was designed to test these hypotheses as well as a prediction that derives from them, namely that girls' enjoyment of sporting activities may account for little unique variance in self-esteem after controlling for the effects of sports participation on such contributors to self-worth as physical competence, a favorable body image, and a heightened sense of masculinity. . . .

Perceived Benefits from Sports Improve Self-Esteem

Previous research on the psychosocial impact for girls of participating in sporting activities is limited and somewhat inconsistent. Although several investigators have argued that sports participation can have a salutary effect on girls' self-esteem, the resulting sport–self-esteem relationships are typically modest and subject to qualification.

One potential shortcoming of previous research is that it typically fails to consider the "quality" of girls' sports experience, that is, how much girls enjoy the sporting activities they undertake. Given that enjoyment is the most frequently cited reason that participants list for partaking in sports, we chose to evaluate a mediating/moderating model that specifies that girls who enjoy sports would benefit psychosocially from their participation and that, at lower levels of enjoyment, continued sports participation may have a negative impact on self-esteem. Our data were consistent with these premises. Not only did sports participation predict sports enjoyment which, in turn, predicted girls' self-esteem, but the marginally significant positive relationship between sports participation and self-esteem became significantly negative after we controlled for the influence of sports enjoyment. Thus, consistent with our model, these outcomes indicate that (1) earlier sports participation fosters self-esteem to the extent that girls enjoy their sporting activities, but (2) could actually undermine the self-worth of girls who find sporting activities less enjoyable.

Our next concern was to explore some potentially important reasons why girls differ in their enjoyment of sports and to determine whether sports enjoyment might make a unique contribution to girls' self-esteem after controlling for the effects of those factors that might contribute to their enjoyment of sporting activities. There are, of course, a multitude of reasons why girls might enjoy sports. In this project, we focused on three sports-related "benefits" that had, in previous research, totally mediated the positive relationship between girls' earlier sports participation and later self-esteem: perceived physical competence, favorability of body image, and masculinity. As expected, each of these proposed contributors to sports enjoyment predicted precollege sports enjoyment and self-esteem during the college years in bivariate analyses. Moreover, each made unique contributions to self-esteem after we controlled for the main effect of precollege sports participation. Finally, our analyses revealed that the sports enjoyment variable did not account for any variance in participants' self-esteem after we controlled for precollege sports participation and such presumed sports-related benefits as increased physical competence, a more favorable body image, and an enhanced sense of masculinity. This finding was anticipated and simply reflects, we believe, that (1) girls enjoy sports to the extent that they perceive themselves as benefiting in some way from sporting activities, and (2) the perceived benefits, rather then enjoyment per se, explains any positive effect of earlier sports participation on the self-esteem of college women.

Limitations of the Present Research

Clearly, this is a correlational study that relies on retrospective reports of prior sports participation and does not conclusively

establish that involvement in sporting activities is causally related to either changes in self-esteem or to the variables presumed to mediate the relationship between sports participation
and self-esteem. Accuracy of retrospective reports can always
be questioned. Although in this project we did not measure
how involved our participants were as collegians in sporting
activities, we can point to data from prior samples drawn
from the same population as our participants that indicate
that retrospective reports of *precollege* sports participation reliably predict college self-esteem and current perceptions of
physical competence, body image, and masculinity, whereas
measures of participants' *college* sports participation do not.
This provides some evidence that our measure of precollege
sports participation was not merely a stand-in for current
sports participation. And, unlike college students' reports of
global self-esteem, earlier participants' retrospective reports of
high school self-esteem were *not* significantly correlated in
previous research with their reports of body image, physical
competence, or masculinity during the college years. . . .

We also wish to caution against treating the experiences of
our highly educated and predominantly White samples as the
"norm" and failing to consider that any psychosocial impact
of sports participation may reliably differ for young women
from other educational and racial/ethnic backgrounds. Indeed,
racial/ethnic variations in women's body image and endorse-
ment of gender-typed traits, are reasons to suspect that any
effect of sport participation on self-esteem could vary across
populations and that our findings may not be at all "norma-
tive" for Women of Color. Thus, future researchers might
strive to oversample participants from minority groups and to
treat the diverse racial/ethnic and socioeconomic backgrounds
of study participants as integral to model building rather than
simply assuming that a middle-class cultural context represents the norm for all young women.

Ways in Which Sports Negatively Affect Girls

- *Teenage girls experience a crisis of confidence.* Studies confirm what we as women know from our own experiences as teenagers: that girls suffer a severe crisis in confidence and larger drop in self-esteem during adolescence than boys (who *gain* self-confidence as they mature). As a result, girls are more likely than boys to quit sports and other challenging activities because they don't view themselves as being good enough.

- *Poor coaching.* Of the eleven reasons cited by girls in a 1988 study as to why they dropped out of sports, the fourth highest was that the coach was a poor teacher; number nine was that the coach played favorites. Coaches who berate and belittle girls turn sports into such a hurtful, harmful experience that dropping out becomes for many a way to avoid further damage to their self-esteem.

- *Teenage girls still think sports are unfeminine.* Back when I was in high school it was not real cool for a girl to be a jock. That is why I didn't go out for basketball my senior year even though it was one of my best sports. Sadly, it is still mostly true today. High school girls interviewed by Rosalind Wiseman for her best-selling book *Queen Bees and Wannabes* said girls can be athletic and have high social status but only if they have thin, "feminine" bodies, and that a large, "masculine" build was unacceptable (which is why many excellent female athletes worry about getting bulky if they lift weights).

Brooke de Lench, "Not Bad for a Girl," Home Team Advantage: The Critical Role of Mothers in Youth Sports, *2006.*

Dislike of Sports Can Undermine Self-Esteem

Despite its limitations, the present research clearly extends existing knowledge by (1) proposing how the quality of girls' sporting experiences (as indexed by sports enjoyment) and specific correlates of these evaluative judgments might influence the relationship between sports participation and self-esteem and (2) generating some plausible support for this model. Our findings also provide some clues about why the apparent psychosocial impacts of sports participation are modest in scope. Simply stated, sporting activities affect different girls in different ways. Sports participation appears to foster the self-esteem of girls who enjoy sporting activities because they perceive themselves as benefiting in some ways by their participation. But in the absence of these positive outcomes, participating in sporting activities may have little psychosocial impact or could actually undermine self-worth. How? For some participants, social comparisons undertaken during sporting activities may highlight just how physically uncoordinated or incapable they are—an inference that may undermine their enjoyment of sports and their sense of global self-worth. Other girls, who may be facing increased pressures to conform to gender-stereotyped behaviors—pressures that are common among adolescent girls—may derive little psychosocial benefit from sporting activities if they are concerned about the non-traditionality of their behavior as participants in a masculine activity or about others' potentially negative reactions to it.

The finding that sports participation might actually undermine the self-worth of some girls has implications for physical educators, parents, or anybody else who might encourage girls to partake in sporting activities. The goal, we believe, should be to find ways of illustrating to participants the *benefits* they might incur from sports-enhanced physical capabilities, weight control, learning to be more appropriately assertive, or even that their efforts, no matter how minor, might contribute in important ways to team objectives and shared goals. Accordingly, gym classes and formal team sports might prove beneficial to larger numbers of girls if educators, coaches, and parents were to emphasize and to devise ways to measure and illustrate the physical and psychological gains derived from formal and informal sporting activities, and to concentrate less on the outcomes of competitive sports or the physical deficiencies of the less athletic girls under their tutelage. In short, we believe that there are steps that adults can take to highlight how girls can profit from participating in sports so that more of them will enjoy such activities, remain physically active, and reap both physical and psychosocial benefits from their participation.

> *"More than 40% of female athletes in grades 9–12 reported ever using sport supplements, while 18% reported current use."*

Sport Supplement Use Is Common Among Female Athletes

Mike Perko, Todd Bartee, and Mike Dunn

Mike Perko is an associate professor and the chair of health sciences at the University of North Carolina at Wilmington; Todd Bartee is an associate professor of health education and promotion at the University of Wyoming at Laramie; Mike Dunn is an associate professor of public health at East Tennessee State University in Johnson City. In the following viewpoint, the authors address the high number of young female athletes who report taking dietary supplements to enhance sports performance by recommendation of friends and family members. Girl athletes make decisions about these substances based on marketing and media information and are unaware of the medical dangers.

Mike Perko, Todd Bartee, and Mike Dunn, "Girls Gone Wild: Girls as the Next Target Market for Sports Dietary Supplements," *The New P.E. & Sports Dimension*, April 2004. Reproduced by permission.

As you read, consider the following questions:

1. As the authors explain, why are marketers and the media able to influence young female athletes to the degree that they do?

2. How does the 1994 Congressional Dietary Supplement Health and Education Act protect the manufacturers of sports enhancer products, in the authors' view?

3. According to the authors, how do girls' reasons for using performance enhancers change as they age?

It's a great time to be a female athlete. Never in the history of sports and athletics have females and especially young girls had the opportunity to participate at every level of sport. In 2003, more than 7 million young athletes played sports at the high school level, the highest number ever seen. The largest percentage of new participants was young girls with over 49,000 girls going out for sports over the previous year, as opposed to 28,000 new male participants. The first surveys, begun in 1971, showed over 3 million boys played organized sports as opposed to only 294,000 for girls; today, current totals equal almost 4 million for boys and almost 3 million for girls!

An Evolving Culture

If you were a male born after 1950, you knew exactly what was expected of you as you entered your first few years in Little League, Pee Wee hockey, and youth soccer. The male sports culture in America has been firmly established for half a century, and expectations for little boys growing up are woven into every community and neighborhood from coast to coast. Not so for little girls. Clearly from a sports perspective, girls born today have tremendous opportunities that their moms did not have. As a girl you can grow up and play professional football, soccer, basketball, baseball, and ice hockey.

Why Girls Use Performance Enhancers

Issue	Number of Respondents	Mean	Median	Mode
Pressure to win	122	1.93	2	1
Self-induced competitive pressures	122	2.02	2	1
Competitive level	122	2.17	2	1
Conscious or unconscious pressure by coaches	122	2.47	2	3
Issues relating to body image	122	2.69	3	3
Peer pressure by teammates	122	2.92	3	3
Pressure by school	122	3.10	3	3
Societal pressures	122	3.25	3	3
Curiosity/experimentation	122	3.34	3	3

The mean, median, and mode columns represent the importance of the issues on a scale of 1 (very important) to 5 (most unimportant).

TAKEN FROM: Barbara Fralinger et al., "Female Athletes and Performance-Enhancer Usage," *Journal of College Teaching & Learning*, December 2007.

You can wrestle. You can box. But while the culture of girls and women in sport is evolving, it has not yet engrained itself into being a "norm." As such, influences other than established ones are playing a huge role in guiding the mindset of the female athlete. Influences such as Nike, Reebok, and other entities are being allowed to shape the notion of what a girl athlete looks like. Entering that marketplace, with millions of new female athletes to target, are the sport dietary supplement companies.

The sources of information that college women report as most popular only exacerbate this marketing scheme. Magazines and product labels (17.1% and 14.7%, respectively) were two of the top sources of information reported. Additionally, friends (19.9%) and parents (16.4%) were the other top sources of information, of which neither group is probably consulting the professional research for their information but are also getting their information from the popular media. Friends were also reported to be who recommended supplement use the most (18%). It is frightening but not unexpected to think that messages created to sell products are shaping the sports culture for female athletes of today and the future.

Current headlines today report on cheating in baseball, track and field, and other sports by athletes who have supposedly taken a performance enhancer such as Androstendione (Andro) or similar sport supplement products. Legal and easily obtainable, sport dietary supplements fall under the guidelines established by the 1994 US Congress when they passed the Dietary Supplement Health and Education Act (DSHEA). The DSHEA effectively states that dietary supplement products cannot be removed from the marketplace unless they are proven to be a health hazard. In essence, the federal government has to show that these products are dangerous, not the maker of the product. This recently happened with the banning of Ephedra, which took seven years and multiple deaths to achieve. Unfortunately, there are 2,999 more products still on the market. Similar, but not as drastic, steps have recently been taken with Andro as a number of manufacturers of products containing this ingredient have been requested to stop distribution due to its potential negative side effects. It is important to note however that although Andro is now considered a "steroid precursor" it still remains an unregulated dietary supplement.

Health Risks Increase with Sport Supplements

So, are young female athletes taking purported performance enhancing supplements such as Andro and Creatine? You bet. Survey data suggest that the current focus in research on young male athletes may be ignoring a population that is emerging as a huge consumer base. More than 40% of female athletes in grades 9–12 reported ever using sport supplements, while 18% reported current use. They also tend to take sport supplements for more than sports performance. Data collected with high school female student-athletes suggest that the most popular reasons reported for using sport supplements were for better health and to increase energy levels (47.3%). Other popular reasons for use were to lose weight (37.2%), look better (21.4%), and play sports better (19.4%).

Interestingly, data collected with female college students suggested that as students get older their main reasons for using supplements may change to gaining muscle size (47.7%). Other reasons reported were similar to responses given by high school female athletes including increasing energy (46.6%), general health (44.4%), and losing weight (29.1%). In addition to assessing the reasons for use, it is equally important to assess the influencing power of significant mentors. It has been reported that parents are a stronger influence compared to athletic trainers and coaches among female athletics.

As such, parents may influence their daughter's use of a supplement by suggesting that the product will give one a competitive edge in athletics and that they will be proud if their daughter is on the team. This can result in dangerous consequences (i.e., kidney failure, hypertension, heart condition, death) since parents usually have low amounts of knowledge of supplements and quite possibly are not consulting any professional source for their information but using what they hear from the media to influence their daughter's intentions to use supplements.

What to Do?

The question is: Do we care that parents and coaches are promoting the use of supplements to female athletes as early as 10 years of age? Do we care that none of these supplements have been tested on adolescents or children? Do we care whether or not young women may grow up with a "winning is everything" attitude or an attitude that supports enjoyment, camaraderie, fair-play, and hard work? Do we want young people to look for unjustified short-cuts and magic bullets to increase sport performance and look better? Or do we want young people to value the true benefits of effective training techniques, proper nutrition, and making the most of their abilities?

There has never been a better time to discuss these products than in the current environment. Unfortunately, most of the conversations will revolve around the male use of supplements. Let's start the conversation here about females.

"Recent studies offer further evidence
that [steroid] use is rare in women and
even rarer in girls."

Steroid Use Among Female Athletes Is Overreported

Gen Kanayama, et al.

Gen Kanayama is from the Boston Psychiatry Laboratory at McLean Hospital, affiliated with Harvard Medical School. His co-authors work there or at the Channing Laboratory in the division of adolescent medicine at the Children's Hospital, also affiliated with Harvard Medical School. The authors of the following viewpoint claim that the alarming statistics about girls using anabolic steroids—reported as high as 7.3 percent of ninthgraders—are generated from poor survey questions and falsepositive answers. They propose a much lower figure, possibly 0.1 percent, of females who have used anabolic steroids in their lifetimes.

As you read, consider the following questions:

1. Why do the authors believe the steroid use rate generated from the Growing Up Today study is reliable?

2. What rates of steroid use among female adolescents in Brazil and Sweden were reported?

3. What recommendation do the authors make to prevent false-positive responses on future surveys of anabolic-androgenic steroid use?

Many men use illicit anabolic-androgenic steroids (AAS) to gain muscle for athletics or appearance. Women, by contrast, would seem unlikely to want to use AAS, since they are less likely to desire muscularity, and also risk masculinizing effects from these drugs. Surprisingly, however, the Centers for Disease Control (CDC) recently reported "lifetime illegal steroid use" in 7.3% of ninth-grade American girls—sparking media warnings of a possible crisis of AAS use among girls. In June 2005, the House Government Reform Committee of the United States Congress held a public hearing regarding AAS abuse by women and girls. Subsequent media coverage has continued to suggest, despite some criticism, that AAS use among American teenage girls is widespread.

Are these concerns justified? Below, we suggest that the reported prevalence of AAS use among girls is often greatly inflated by false-positive responses to survey questions, and that true AAS use among girls is rare.

A Review of Major Studies

Four large national surveys have assessed the lifetime prevalence of AAS use in American teenage girls—yielding grossly discrepant estimates, ranging from 0.1% to 7.3%. These discrepancies cannot reasonably be attributed to sampling differences, because the surveys showed no comparable differences in their prevalence estimates for other drugs, such as cannabis. The discrepancies also cannot be explained by secular trends in the prevalence of AAS use, since all but one of the studies were performed within the last few years. Therefore, to better explain the discrepancies, we examine differences in study methodology.

The CDC study—The CDC surveys ask a single question about use of "steroid pills or shots without a doctor's prescription." But this question has several deficiencies. First, it does not specify *anabolic-androgenic* steroids as opposed to corticosteroids; therefore a girl using, say, prednisone for poison ivy might answer positively, defeating the question's intent. Second, the phrase "without a doctor's prescription" implies that doctors typically prescribe "steroids"—whereas doctors actually almost never prescribe AAS to girls. Third, respondents may erroneously think that "steroids" are present in over-the-counter sports supplements, such as protein powders, amino acids, creatine, or supplements with names suggestive of AAS. Fourth, the question asks "how many times" the respondent has taken "steroids," (i.e., "1 or 2 times," "3 to 9 times," etc.). But this again is misleading, because unlike other illicit drugs, AAS are not taken on individual "times," but instead for a course measured in weeks or months. For all of these reasons, respondents may misinterpret the "steroid" question and give false-positive responses. Note that these four problems do not affect questions regarding other drugs of abuse; questions regarding, say, cocaine or marijuana are unambiguous. . . .

The Monitoring the Future Study—Unlike the CDC question, the Monitoring the Future (MTF) study question mentions the specific term "anabolic steroids," and adds that "steroids" are used for muscle development. Like the CDC question, however, the MTF question still misleadingly implies that doctors typically prescribe AAS, or might "tell you to take them," and that AAS are taken on individual "times." Also, the question does not specifically caution respondents that AAS should not be confused with corticosteroids or sports supplements. Overall, then, this question should still yield some false positives, but fewer than the CDC—and as predicted, the MTF study indeed produces lower estimates.

Studies That Eliminate Variables Produce Much Lower Estimates

The Growing Up Today Study—Unlike the CDC and MTF studies, the Growing Up Today (GUT) study places its "steroid" question last in a series of seven questions regarding substances typically used for muscle gains, fat loss, or athletic performance. Therefore, having just answered the six previous questions, respondents are well cued that "anabolic/injectable steroids" refers to AAS as opposed to, say, corticosteroids. Respondents are also unlikely to confuse "steroids" with over-the-counter supplements such as protein or creatine, since they have already answered separate questions about these categories. These features should minimize false-positive responses—and therefore the GUT study's 0.1% estimate for lifetime AAS use among teenage girls seems likely accurate. . . .

The National Household Survey—Unlike the previous studies, the National Household Survey (NHS) utilized trained interviewers, rather than anonymous questionnaires. With an interviewer present to provide clarification and query subjects about equivocal responses, one would expect few false-positives—and indeed, for girls aged 14–19, the NHS estimated the lifetime prevalence of AAS use at only 0.1%. Even this figure might still include some false-positives, however, because approximately 95% of girls were not asked verbally about AAS, but simply answered a written questionnaire in the presence of the interviewer. Although the written question appropriately uses the term "anabolic steroids," it fails to caution that AAS should not be confused with corticosteroids or sports supplements, and it implies that AAS are drugs typically prescribed by doctors—factors conducive to false-positive re-

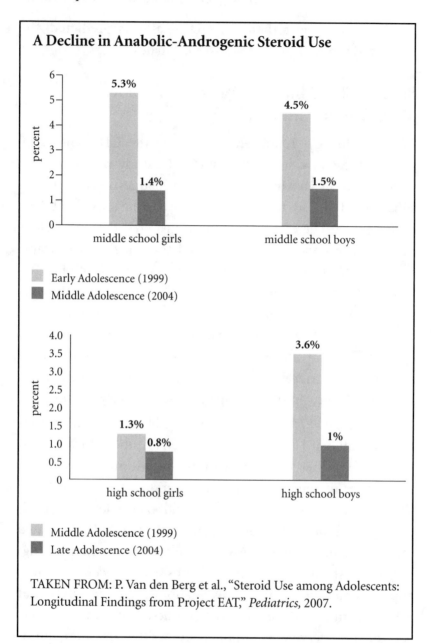

A Decline in Anabolic-Androgenic Steroid Use

TAKEN FROM: P. Van den Berg et al., "Steroid Use among Adolescents: Longitudinal Findings from Project EAT," *Pediatrics*, 2007.

sponses, as discussed above. Therefore, the NHS figure, low as it is, might still overestimate of the true prevalence of AAS use in teenage girls.

It might be argued that the NHS estimate is out of date, because this survey has not assessed AAS use among teenagers since 1994. However, longitudinal data, such as the annual MTF figures, show no marked rise in AAS use between 1994 and 2005—suggesting that the 1994 NHS figures are still applicable. It might also be argued that the NHS produced false negatives because respondents were unwilling to disclose illicit AAS use to an interviewer. But this argument also seems implausible, since the NHS produced substantial prevalence estimates for other illicit drugs, such as cannabis, despite the lack of anonymity.

In summary, upon inspecting the national studies above, it appears that among American girls 14–19, the true lifetime prevalence of AAS use is likely about 0.1%, as estimated by the GUT and NHS studies, and that the higher estimates in the CDC and MTF studies are attributable to false-positive responses. . . .

High School Surveys Mirror Major Studies

Many additional studies have estimated the prevalence of AAS use in more local samples of teenagers. . . . All of these studies used anonymous or confidential questionnaires; none, to our knowledge, provided an explicit definition of AAS, and none cautioned respondents that AAS should not be confused with corticosteroids or sports supplements. Several additional studies utilized CDC data from individual regions; these studies by definition have the same flaws as the national CDC studies already discussed. . . . Overall, therefore, it would follow that most estimates of AAS use among high-school girls should be greatly inflated by false-positives.

A notable exception . . . is the study of [Diane L.] Elliot and colleagues (2004), who found lifetime AAS use in only 0.1% of 928 female high-school athletes. Athletes might be expected to exhibit greater AAS use than girls in general—yet Elliott and colleagues found a far lower prevalence than the other surveys of girls as a whole. There is a likely explanation for this difference: athletes, answering a questionnaire focusing on performing-enhancing substances, would rarely misinterpret the term "steroid"—thus minimizing false-positive responses. The study's results also seem unlikely to be seriously biased by false-negative responses from genuine AAS users who denied use—since respondents readily acknowledged substantial use of other drugs, such as marijuana and diet pills. Therefore, the study's 0.1% estimate for lifetime AAS use among girls seems reasonable.

Evidence from Other Studies Involving Women

Two other recent studies offer further evidence that AAS use is rare in women and even rarer in girls. [One study] (2001) gave anonymous questionnaires to 511 clients at five gymnasiums, including two "hard-core" gymnasiums frequented by competitive bodybuilders. Since AAS use is usually associated with strength training, one would expect gymnasiums, especially "hard-core" gymnasiums, to show high concentrations of AAS users. Indeed, AAS use was reported by 18 (5.4%) of 334 men, but none of 177 women.

In the other [2000] study, [researchers] systematically recruited and interviewed female AAS users; this was the only published study in the last decade, to our knowledge, reporting direct interviews of women using AAS. The investigators advertised extensively for subjects in gymnasiums—a method that had previously yielded ample numbers of male AAS users—but found only 25 female AAS users in three metropolitan areas over a two-year period. Of these, none reported AAS use prior to age 20.

Indeed, to our knowledge, no scientific paper in the last 10 years has described a girl or woman, personally interviewed, who reported AAS use prior to age 20. Considering that approximately 23,000,000 American girls reached age 20 between 1996 and 2006, and allowing that even 0.5% of these girls used AAS before age 20, then there would be 115,000 American women, presently age 20–30, who first used AAS as teenagers. If so, it would seem remarkable that none has been described in the scientific literature.

Studies from Other Countries

We are aware of only one national survey of teenage AAS use outside of the United States: [researchers in 2004] studied 48,155 Brazilian students, using a survey question designed to minimize false positives—providing specific examples of nine representative AAS widely used in Brazil (Androlone, Anabolex, etc.), and asking respondents who answered "yes" to name the AAS that they had used. Only those naming a genuine AAS were scored positive. For students age 14–19, the lifetime prevalence was 3.1% for boys, but only 0.4% for girls.

Two other large overseas studies, though not national, are also instructive. [Sverker] Nilsson et al. (2001) surveyed 5,827 students aged 16–17 in a county in Sweden, using an instrument that included descriptive information to clarify the term "anabolic steroids." Although 84 (2.9%) of the 2,785 boys reported AAS use, no cases were found among the 3,042 girls. By contrast, [D.J.] Handelsman and [L.] Gupta (1997) surveyed 13,355 high-school students in southeastern Australia and reported AAS use in 3.2% of boys and 1.2% of girls. The Australian questionnaire, however, exhibited many of the same deficits as the CDC questionnaire described above, namely asking about use of "steroids" without cautioning respondents that "steroids" should not be confused with corticosteroids or sports supplements. Thus the Australian survey, unlike the Brazilian and Swedish surveys, likely generated many false-positive responses.

We believe that quoted prevalence estimates of AAS use are often greatly inflated by false-positive responses to imprecise questions regarding "steroids" on anonymous questionnaires. Our analysis suggests that the true lifetime prevalence of AAS use among American teenage girls is well below 0.5%, and possibly only 0.1%. This impression should be tested in subsequent surveys using questions carefully designed to eliminate false-positive responses as described above. Ideally, such questions should first be tested and validated via follow-up interviews. However, since AAS use is uncommon, a fully adequate validation study might require a denominator of thousands of respondents, making it impractical. Nevertheless, false-positive responses could certainly be minimized by formulating survey questions that 1) caution respondents that AAS should not be confused with corticosteroids or over-the-counter nutritional supplements; 2) provide examples of commonly used AAS; and 3) require respondents to name the AAS that they have used, as in the Brazilian study above.

These conclusions have important implications for public health policy. If AAS use is indeed rare among teenage girls, then it may be irrational to devote extensive resources in this area; resources targeted at prevention of AAS use may be better concentrated on males, for whom the prevalence and hazards of AAS use are better documented.

Periodical Bibliography

The following articles have been selected to supplement the diverse views presented in this chapter.

Patricia van der Berg, et al.
"Steroid Use Among Adolescents: Longitudinal Findings from Project EAT," *Pediatrics*, March 2007.

Diane L. Elliot, et al.
"Cross-Sectional Study of Female Students Reporting Anabolic Steroid Use," *Archives of Pediatric and Adolescent Medicine*, June 2007.

Nanci Hellmich
"Athletes' Hunger to Win Fuels Eating Disorders," *USA Today*, February 5, 2006.

Mary Jo Kane and Nicole M. LaVoi
"Developing Physically Active Girls," The 2007 Tucker Center Research Report, 2007. www.cehd.umn.edu/tuckercenter.

Mary E. Pritchard and Gregory S. Wilson
"Factors Influencing Body Image in Female Adolescent Athletes," *Women in Sport & Physical Activity Journal*, Spring 2005.

Robin Roenker
"'Girls on the Run' Program Builds Confidence as It Encourages Exercise," *Lexington Herald-Leader*, April 29, 2009.

Harriet Salbach, et al.
"Body Image and Attitudinal Aspects of Eating Disorders in Rhythmic Gymnasts," *Psychopathology*, September 2007.

Alan Schwarz
"Girls Are Often Neglected Victims of Concussions," *New York Times*, October 2, 2007.

Shubha Singh, et al.
"Gymnastics-Related Injuries to Children Treated in Emergency Departments in the United States, 1990–2005," *Pediatrics*, April 2008.

Byron L. Zamboanga and Lindsay S. Ham
"Alcohol Expectancies and Context-Specific Drinking Behaviors Among Female College Athletes," *Behavior Therapy*, June 2008.

OPPOSING
VIEWPOINTS®
SERIES

CHAPTER 3

Do Schools Support Girls' Sports Programs?

Chapter Preface

"Separate but equal" is a phrase with a long history in the United States. An artifact from the era of racial segregation, it became an official part of the judicial system in the U.S. Supreme Court ruling *Plessy v. Ferguson*, an 1896 case that decided in favor of maintaining separate train cars for black and white travelers so long as the train cars were of equal quality. In 1954, the Supreme Court reversed its stance on "separate but equal" in the *Brown v. Board of Education of Topeka* case, which was the culmination of a series of legal claims that separate schools led to unequal quality. U.S. schools are now legally compelled to accept students of all races.

Nearly two decades after the *Brown* case, Congress passed Title IX of the Education Amendments of 1972, known commonly as Title IX. This law states, "No person in the United States shall, on the basis of sex, be excluded in, denied the benefits of, or be subjected to discrimination under any educational program or activity receiving Federal assistance." It addresses gender discrimination in all school programs (including academic subjects), but it is known mostly for guaranteeing girls' access to school sports programs. Since the passing of Title IX, girls' participation in sports has increased nearly tenfold, and schools devote many resources to achieving and maintaining compliance. Great care is taken to ensure girls playing sports have their own equipment, their own locker rooms, and their own teams. Larger schools even have separate athletic directors for the girls' sports program. Girls and boys' sports organizations run on equal tracks, but separate ones.

There is no biological reason to educate people of different races separately, but sex-segregated athletic teams are considered perfectly natural, especially considering that the average male is stronger and more powerful than the average female. The concept of "separate but equal" is accepted in athletics departments; when girls and boys receive equal portions of available sports resources, there are few complaints about the "separate" part. It is almost universally assumed that pitting girls against boys in competition would undermine girls' chances to succeed in sports at all and would reduce the top female athletes to mere second-string, back-up players in a male game.

A new controversy has arisen, however, regarding separate-but-equal sex-segregated physical education classes. Although boys and girls may attend physical education classes at the same time on the same field, many schools assign all the girls in the class to one teacher and all the boys to another. Girls and boys sometimes even receive separate curricula. Separating male and female athletes in competition is one thing, but some educators and coaches now argue that gender-divided physical education classes negatively affect female students. In the February 2008 issue of the *Journal of Physical Education, Recreation, and Dance*, James Hannon and Skip Williams of the department of exercise and sport science at the University of Utah in Salt Lake City analyze data about the quality of girls-only physical education classes. Although many teachers believe providing girls the opportunity to learn sports skills with other girls (instead of with generally stronger, more powerful boys) gives them more time to practice and more confidence to do so, some research suggests girls in girls-only physical education classes perform with less vigor and spend less time with elevated heart rates than girls in co-educational classes. These girls in co-educational classes are working harder, learning more, and honing their skills more sharply. The schools with sex-segregated physical education classes may equally support girls' and boys' interscholastic competitive teams with time, money, and practice spaces, but they may also be insufficiently supporting the health and athletic development of the girls in recreational and educational activity programs by separating them from the boys in their class.

The following chapter addresses the different ways that school administrators and coaches provide girls with opportunities to participate in sports and examines the successes or failures of their attempts to achieve equality between boys' and girls' sports programs despite the segregation by sex of the participants.

"*[Athletic directors] strive to make sure that all their athletes are given equal opportunities to participate in the athletic program and be successful at it.*"

Schools Are Complying with Title IX Regulations

Becky Vest and Gerald Masterson

Becky Vest is the assistant coach of the Lady Bobcats, the women's basketball team at College of the Ozarks in Point Lookout, Missouri. Gerald Masterson is a professor in the health, physical education and recreation department at Missouri State University at Springfield. In the following viewpoint, the authors summarize the findings of their survey of high schools and colleges regarding the steps that athletic directors have taken to ensure equality of opportunity for female and male athletes in school sports programs. According to Vest and Masterson, athletic directors have found many ways to demonstrate compliance to Title IX regulations and increase levels of participation among girls and women.

Becky Vest and Gerald Masterson, "Title IX and Its Effects on Sports Programs in High School and Collegiate Athletics," *Coach and Athletic Director*, vol. 77, December 2007, pp. 60–62. Copyright © 2007 Scholastic Inc. Reproduced by permission of Scholastic Inc.

As you read, consider the following questions:

1. How have official Title IX regulations affected the pursuit of funding for women's athletic programs, according to the authors?

2. What has happened to the numbers of female participants in sports programs over the past decade, in the authors' view?

3. How do the authors assert the addition of female programs to athletic budgets has affected the funding of male sports programs?

Title IX has made a colossal impact on school sport. It has forever changed budgeting and participation numbers between males and females and opened up many opportunities for women.

After an intensive investigation of the schools on the high school and NAIA [National Association of Intercollegiate Athletics] (college) levels, I believe I can speak with authority on how they have adapted to meet the mandates of Title IX: What changes they have made, the overall impact of Title IX, and the variances and similarities in the legal decisions.

Representative Edith Green of Oregon introduced the beginning of the sex bias issue in education and the hearing, which led to the first legislative step of passing Title IX.

In 1971, five different bills were introduced in the House, Senate, and White House proposing to end sex discrimination in education. Their general sentiment was that sex discrimination should cease, but the legislatures could not come to an agreement on the best way to do it.

It took several months for the House-Senate Conference Committee to settle on the differences in all the House and Senate education bills, 11 of which addressed sex discrimination. Title IX was adopted by the House-Senate Conference Committee and then sent to the full Senate. The Senate approved it on May 22, 1972. From the Senate, it went to the House, where it was passed on June 8.

On June 23, it was signed by President [Richard] Nixon and it went into effect on July 1. The final regulations were issued on July 20, 1974, and on May 27, 1975 President Gerald Ford signed them. They were then presented to Congress for review.

How Title IX Affects Sports Programs

Title IX of the Education Amendments Act of 1972 is a federal law that states: "No person in the United States shall, on the basis of sex, be excluded from participation in, be denied the benefits of, or be subjected to discrimination under any education program or activity receiving Federal financial assistance."

Title IX is applied to athletics in several ways. First, separate teams for boys and girls must be provided; otherwise, students of both sexes must be allowed to try out for the same team. Secondly, equal opportunities must be provided for both sexes in the educational institution in terms of competitive training facilities, equipment and supplies, facilities for practice and games, medical and training services, coaching and academic tutoring, travel allowances, housing and dining facilities, compensation of coaches, and publicity.

In addition, Title IX guidelines provide that expenditures on men's and women's sports be proportional to the number of men and women participating. This guideline is applied to athletic scholarships, recruitment, as well as equipment, supplies, travel, recruiting, and publicity. Finally, Title IX requires colleges and universities to take specific steps to provide additional competitive sport opportunities for women.

Title IX Brought Balance to Sports

According to the U.S. Department of Education and its [1997] publication "Title IX: 25 Years of Progress," there has been a dramatic increase in the number of girls and women who participate in athletics. In 1971, less than 300,000 high school girls played inter-scholastic sports; in 1997 that number had risen to 2.4 million.

Two years after Title IX was enacted, approximately 50,000 men and less than 80 women received athletic scholarships to colleges and universities.

By 1997, one-third of all the scholarship money was going to women.

To further check the current impact of Title IX, I conducted interviews with current athletic directors [ADs] at both small and large high schools as well as from NAIA colleges. I asked 10 questions on the effect that Title IX has had on their school and athletic programs and also asked the ADs what types of changes they have made in order to comply with Title IX. I interviewed athletic directors in order to grasp the similarities and differences in the way they dealt with Title IX and the similarities and differences between small and large high schools and colleges.

The answers were characteristically broad. There was little difference in the impact of Title IX among high school athletic programs. Most schools stated that they provided female athletes with the same opportunities as male athletes, although one large high school stated that Title IX did come into play when adding a new sport.

The colleges said Title IX gave them a platform to stand on when requesting more money for women's athletics and they seemed to emphasize the importance of budgeting for women's athletics.

One NAIA college reported that Title IX impacted them very little because they were already offering equal opportunities to their athletes, prior to Title IX.

How Schools Make Decisions About Compliance

Important decisions have to be made when schools have to equalize the number of men and women's athletics. One of the questions asked was what types of decisions had to be made in terms of cutting and adding sports.

It was surprising that none of the high schools or colleges I surveyed had cut a single men's sport to equalize the gender of the teams. Every high school and NAIA college that I talked to had added one or more female athletic teams in order to make it fair.

One strategy that came from a large high school was to look for programs that had both a girl's and a boy's team in the same sport. When forced to cut athletic teams because of budget, this strategy enabled them to be fair to both genders.

Athletic directors seem to have a variety of policies that determine what sports to cut and what sports to add. One small high school policy is to add or cut sports based on the equality of participation. If one sport is cut or added, it is done by both sexes.

Larger high schools determined adding or cutting based on conference affiliation, cost, revenue, facilities, number of schools in the area that field teams in that sport, and if it meets the needs of their community.

One college AD stated that he would add or cut sports based solely on student interest. Another used an Athletic Committee consisting of school faculty to help reach a decision, and then passed it on for the approval of the administration.

How Have Schools' Efforts Affected Girls' Participation?

Nearly all of the ADs said that Title IX had made no changes in the number of female athletes in recent years. Since the ADs had been at their respective schools for approximately the last 10 years, this meant that Title IX has been successful at those high schools and NAIA colleges; and that male and female athletic participation numbers have stabilized over the past ten years.

One might have expected a sharp increase in female participation that put them near equal to male participation numbers in recent years. But it appears that the numbers stabilized somewhat.

Of the schools surveyed, only one monitored participation numbers. It required each head coach to make an end-of-the-season report, which included participation numbers. The schools used the report to monitor the stability of each sport, not for Title IX compliance.

All the schools questioned, however, make sure to offer equal opportunities for male and females. Title IX does not order schools to have the same number of male and female athletes; but it does mandate that all have equal opportunities.

Budgeting for Increased Numbers of Female Athletes

High schools have a different approach to the financial effect of Title IX. Some schools claim that Title IX has had no financial effect on them at all. Other schools state that when they add sports, they take money away from other activities, so that each sport gets a smaller piece of the pie.

No ADs mentioned that fundraising was an option they used to make money for their program. High schools do not have scholarship money, so their biggest concern is reducing the money given to other sports and use the savings to finance equal sport offerings.

The colleges viewed Title IX as a way to recruit student athletes with the charisma to put people in seats.

One way high schools and colleges may save money is by changing their game schedule. For example: Scheduling games closer to home.

Publicity Should Promote Sports Teams Equally

Under Title IX, schools are obligated to devote the same amount of publicity to both girls' and boys' sports. However, many schools promote boys' athletic events much more than girls' events. Examples of publicity include:

- School newspaper articles
- Pep rallies
- Cheerleaders, drill teams, pep bands, etc.
- Yearbook coverage
- Public address announcements
- Bulletin boards
- Web site announcements
- School calendars
- Athletic awards and recognition

If varsity cheerleaders perform at boys' games, they should also perform at girls' games. If the school has a homecoming rally for the football team, it should have a similar rally for a girls' team, or include girls' teams in the same rally. It is very important to emphasize girls' sports because there is a long-standing tradition of favoring male teams. Publicizing girls' sports can help eliminate the stereotype that boys' sports are more important, and it can also help boost girls' confidence in themselves. Publicity can also help draw more spectators to girls' sports.

Vicky L. Barker, "Covering All the Bases," Time Out: Does Your School Play Fair? *California Women's Law Center, 2006.*

One small high school and one large high school are in the process of cutting their schedules. The small high school cut back 10% on scheduling and eliminated some long trips.

It seems that most schools will just find the money for their athletic programs rather than reduce the number of games and trips or cut the other athletic programs.

None of the colleges questioned have changed their scheduling in order to save money, and none of the NAIA colleges surveyed cut men's athletic scholarships.

The survey also asked whether men's athletic teams have the same number of scholarships as female athletic teams. Once again, the NAIA colleges were in agreement with their responses. They offer an equal number of scholarships for the same men and women's athletic team. For example, the men's baseball team has the same number of scholarships as the women's softball team.

Ensuring Equal Opportunity

Finally, all of the schools that responded, both high school and college, offer the same number of men's and women's sports in order to maintain an equal playing field. Most of the ADs strive to make sure that all their athletes are given equal opportunities to participate in the athletic program and be successful at it. And they also make sure that the athletic teams are getting all that they are entitled to (locker rooms, equipment and supplies, practice facilities). One NAIA college actually has more women's athletic teams than men's teams.

Summing up, it is apparent that even though Title IX went into effect over 30 years ago, our schools are still continuously striving to broaden and equalize their athletic programs. The problems remain. But one thing has to be conceded:

Though our schools may have different routes to the promised land, they are all on the right path when it comes to carrying out the requirements of Title IX.

> *"Even after more than thirty years of Title IX, women are still not a priority."*

Schools Are Not Complying with Title IX Regulations

Megan Seely

Megan Seely teaches sociology and women's studies at Sierra College in Rocklin, California; she has also served two terms in the California branch of the National Organization for Women (NOW). The following viewpoint is excerpted from her book, Fight like a Girl: How to Be a Fearless Feminist, *a handbook for people interested in feminist history and activism. In the following viewpoint, the author shows that despite the passage of Title IX legislation more than 30 years ago, women's athletic departments are not apportioned or funded as well as those of men, nor do men's teams have to be cut to add women's teams.*

As you read, consider the following questions:

1. According to Seely, what is one side effect of schools selecting "proportionality" to demonstrate compliance with Title IX regulations?

2. As the author reports, how has the number of women coaches changed since the passage of Title IX?

3. What are some examples Seely identifies of gender inequity in sports at the professional level?

Numerous studies, including those done by the California Women's Law Center and the Women's Sports Foundation, show that many women and girls who participate in sports have increased self-esteem, improved academic performance, better scores on standardized tests, higher rates of high school and college graduation, and higher rates of college attendance than their nonathletic female counterparts; they have lower rates of teen pregnancy and are less likely to stay in abusive relationships. Additionally, we know that girls who are involved in sports have a more positive body image and better overall health. Given these results, it is concerning that we don't do a better job at encouraging and supporting girls' athletics. Are we frightened by the prospect of girls defining themselves, feeling strong in their bodies, bench pressing 250, or running a minute mile?

In recent years we have seen a rise in women's professional sports—from the Women's National Basketball Association (WNBA) to the Women's Professional Football League (WPFL)—further providing young women healthy images and models to emulate. But, despite the move into professional sports and the known positive effect that sports have in the lives of women and girls, we are still fighting for equal access, recognition, and funding. In addition to educational equity, Title IX [1972 legislation that prohibits gender discrimination in public programs] seeks to create athletic equity. In fact, athletics is the most immediately visible part of Title IX requirements. Under Title IX, educational institutions must provide equitable athletic opportunities to all students, regardless of sex, in three specific areas: participation, treatment of athletes, and athletic scholarships. In order to evaluate a school's compliance with Title IX in athletics, the Office of Civil Rights established a three-pronged test, and schools must meet one of the three criteria in order to be compliant. The three prongs are these:

1. Proportionality: assessing whether male and female students are participating in athletics proportional in numbers to their enrollment at the school;

2. History: a school must show a history of expanding opportunities in athletics for the underrepresented sex;

3. Meeting interest and abilities: a school must fully meet the interest and abilities of the underrepresented sex.

The Money Is Not Funding Women's Teams

Most schools choose proportionality to test their compliance. Unfortunately, instead of truly ensuring access to athletics, this criterion means that women and girls are often blamed for cuts to men's sports. In response to demands for Title IX compliance, schools often cut men's teams to "make room" for women's teams—thus pitting men against women. The media tell the tragic stories of the men's lacrosse team being axed because those greedy women want a softball team. But what we rarely hear are stories of hotel rooms for football players who are playing at-home games, or the practice of purchasing new uniforms and multiple practice uniforms every season; or examples such as these, found by the Women's Sports Foundation:

• One university spent $300,000 putting lights on a football practice field that has never been used for football practice. It wanted to be able to impress potential recruits.

• One college housed the whole football team in a hotel for the entire preseason football camp because dorms were not available for the last two days and the coach didn't want the interruption. The snack bill alone was $86,000.

• A university dropped its men's swimming and diving program, citing economics. That same university found the means to (1) renovate the outdoor track, (2) renovate the indoor track, including the installation of hydraulic banked turns, (3) build a multifield baseball complex with heating elements under the soil to keep the grass growing year round, (4) add a new row of skyboxes to the football stadium, and (5) install new state of the art turf in the football stadium.

We also rarely hear of the challenges faced by women athletes—challenges like those faced by the women's swim team that has to share parkas between races; or the women's diving team that has to practice in the dark with flashlights after the men's water polo team has finished practicing even though they are off season; or the teams that are told that women's uniforms must be self-funded or that the costs of travel to games are the individual responsibility of team members. We also don't hear about who is awarded the majority of athletic scholarships—"each year male athletes receive $133 million or 36 percent more than female athletes in college athletic scholarships at NCAA [National Collegiate Athletic Association] member institutions." Scholarship awards are often a deciding factor in college attendance. The truth of the matter is that for colleges and universities the issue is about prioritizing—and it is clear that even after more than thirty years of Title IX, women are still not a priority. Despite the assertion that women's sports have caused the demise of men's sports, both women's and men's participation in athletics has increased under Title IX—women's participation in intercollegiate sports increased from 90,000 in the 1981–1982 school year to 163,000 in 1998–1999, and men's participation went from 220,000 to

232,000 in those same years. It is possible to increase the number of women's teams without cutting any men's teams—as 72 percent of schools were able to do between the 1992–1993 and 1999–2000 school years. If we are to believe that girls and women have as much a right to play competitive sports as boys and men, and that the word athlete is not exclusively for men, then we must continue to support Title IX.

Challenges to Title IX and Women's Sports

While gains have been made in women's participation in sports, we still have a way to go before we see true proportionality and representation for women athletes. And, while we have made gains in many areas, we are losing ground in coaching and leadership positions for women. Women coaches are paid less than men and face significant barriers to advancement in their fields. In college athletic programs, women account for only 9 percent of sports information directors, 25 percent of all head athletic trainers, 34 percent of athletic administrators, and a mere 2 percent of the coaches for men's teams. In contrast, men now hold the majority of coaching positions for women's teams. In the 1970s, with the passage of Title IX, 90 percent of women's team were coached by women. Today, only 44 percent of coaches of women's teams are women. A recent study found that a whopping 80 percent of head-coaching jobs created for women's sports since 1998 were filled by men.

On the professional level, we are finally seeing the emergence of women sports stars. Venus and Serena Williams, Annika Sorenstam, Laila Ali, Michelle Kwan, Mia Hamm, Sue Bird, Sheryl Swoops, Lisa Leslie, Diana Taurasi, Natalie Couglin, and the many WNBA, NCAA, and WPFL players all give us heroes to watch in sports. But as in the other arenas in which women serve as heroes, they're neither recognized nor awarded the same status as their male counterparts. The aver-

Juggling the Genders for Equity in Sports

Clearly, gender equity is not part of big-time college sports programs. To move from its current imbalance, athletic administrations have three choices: spend more on women's sports, reduce or eliminate nonrevenue men's sports, or constrict football. . . .[A]thletic departments will continue to add low-cost women's sports such as soccer and crew and cut low-profile men's sports such as wrestling, gymnastics, and baseball. Adding women's sports increases their participation, but it does not move them much closer to gender parity in scholarships or in other forms of economic assistance. . . .

Another solution . . . is for women's sports to generate more revenue. Women's sports programs are at a disadvantage in producing significant revenues for several reasons:

1. Men's intercollegiate sport had a hundred-year head start in building tradition and fan support.

2. . . .[W]omen's sports programs have not been given anything approaching parity in resource allocation.

3. Women's sports are relatively ignored by university sports publicity and promotion staff, local and national newspapers, magazines, and television.

4. Women's sports continue to be trivialized by the schools in the naming of their teams (e.g., Wildkittens), as well as by the emphasis on the looks and nonathletic side of women athletes rather than their performance.

D. Stanley Eitzen, Fair and Foul: Beyond the Myths and Paradoxes of Sport, *3rd ed. Lanham, MD: Rowman & Littlefield Publishers, Inc., 2006.*

age NBA [National Basketball Association] salary in 1999–2000 was 58 percent higher than the average WNBA salary; professional women tennis players make sixty-seven cents for every dollar earned by male tennis players; and in professional golf that number drops to thirty-six cents. Pay inequity in sports is real. For example, based on reported prize winnings, when Venus Williams won the Wimbledon title in 2005, she received 30,000 British pounds, or about $55,000 less than Roger Federer, who won the men's singles the following day. Ironically, most commentators acknowledge that women's tennis is far more exiting to watch than men's—the public seems to agree, as the television ratings for women's tennis are higher than those for men's games. When a man argues for a higher salary, we give him props, sing his praises, and never doubt his worth. When a woman does, we tell her that she is lucky to be playing a sport she loves. When a male sport star is accused of rape, domestic violence, or even murder, we usually allow him to continue playing—and often rearrange his court dates (if there are any) to avoid disrupting the season. But when a woman star poses for *Playboy*, we are outraged at her indecency. You'd think if we were going to hold women to such a higher standard, we'd pay them better!

"Female athletes are participating in higher numbers than ever before."

Title IX Has Increased Girls' Participation in School Sports

R. Vivian Acosta and Linda Jean Carpenter

R. Vivian Acosta and Linda Jean Carpenter are professors emeritae of Brooklyn College in New York. They have been surveying National Collegiate Athletic Association schools and publishing their findings about girls' participation and women's involvement in school sports for thirty-one years. In the following viewpoint, the authors summarize how the numbers of female athletes and female teams have increased since the passage of Title IX in 1972; 2008 had the highest numbers ever. The authors also comment on social, political, and legal changes that have supported this vast change in girls' formal participation in sports.

As you read, consider the following questions:

1. How has the average number of varsity women's teams changed from 1970 to 2008, according to Acosta and Carpenter?

R. Vivian Acosta and Linda Jean Carpenter, "Participation: Commentary," *Women in Intercollegiate Sport: A Longitudinal, National Study, Thirty-One Year Update (1977–2008)*, 2008, pp. 10–11. Copyright © 2008 Acosta/Carpenter. Reproduced by permission.

2. How do the authors assert the numbers of female high school varsity athletes compare to the numbers of female college athletes?

3. In the authors' view, how did the awarding of punitive and compensatory damages in the 1992 *Franklin v. Gwinnett* legal decision support current Title IX regulations?

In 1970, prior to the 1972 enactment of Title IX [legislation that prohibits gender discrimination in public programs] there were only 2.5 women's teams per school. In 2008, there are 8.65.

In 1977–78, the academic year preceding the Title IX mandatory compliance date, the number of varsity sports offered women had grown to 5.61 per school. A decade later, in 1988, the number had grown to 7.31 and another decade later, in 1998 the number had grown to 7.71. At the turn of the [twenty-first] century, the growth continued to 8.14 varsity women's teams per campus and, today, in 2008, there is an average of 8.65 women's varsity teams per campus.

The 2008 average of 8.65 is the highest ever and demonstrates without question that the phrase, "If you build it, they will come," applies to women's athletics programs.

Women's 2008 Participation Is the Highest in History

The number of schools offering women's athletics programs has also grown over the years. So, it might be helpful to look not only at the average number of teams per school, but [also] the absolute number of women's teams offered in NCAA [National Collegiate Athletic Association] member schools. That number, 9,101, is also the highest ever. Indeed, there has been an increase of 399 women's teams in the last two years.

In the decade, the average increase in the number of women's teams per school is well over 2.7 per school. In most locales, the pent-up demand for new women's teams exceeds the number of new teams created.

Under Title IX, a school has three options available with which to demonstrate compliance with the law's requirement for equal opportunity to participate. One of those options is to show a history of upgrading the program of the historically underrepresented sex (female). The measurement of this option is totally subjective but an argument could be made that at least exceeding the average increase in teams over a decade might be a starting place from which to create a yardstick of compliance. In 2008, that would mean that a school created more than 2.7 new teams for women in the past decade.

The massive growth in participation is highlighted by a juxtaposition of the number of female *athletes* participating just a few years before Title IX was enacted to the number of intercollegiate *teams* for women currently found in the nation.

More Than 180,000 Females Are Intercollegiate Athletes

The growth on the college level is, to some degree, paralleled by similar growth on the high school level. Data from the National Federation of State High School Associations show that female athletes are participating in higher numbers than ever before and in 2007 surpass 3 million participants. The growth in the number of female high school participants has occurred without interfering with the growth of male participants which, according to the National Federation of State High School Associations is higher than anytime in the past 29 years. The same is generally true on the college level: participation levels for both males and females have increased over the years. The popularity of specific sports has changed with changing interests, altered feeder systems, facility and financial concerns, and administrative decisions sometimes based on factors unrelated to a particular sport. Nonetheless, the total participation levels for male athletes and female athletes have increased.

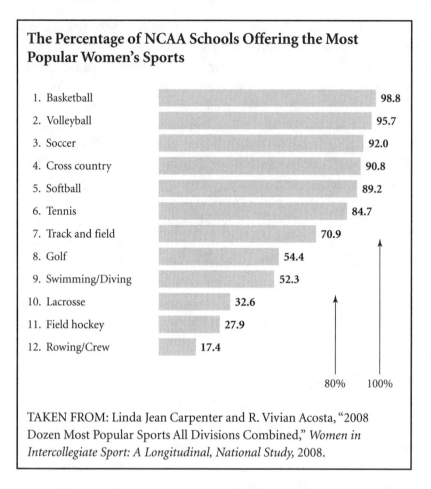

The Percentage of NCAA Schools Offering the Most Popular Women's Sports

1. Basketball — 98.8
2. Volleyball — 95.7
3. Soccer — 92.0
4. Cross country — 90.8
5. Softball — 89.2
6. Tennis — 84.7
7. Track and field — 70.9
8. Golf — 54.4
9. Swimming/Diving — 52.3
10. Lacrosse — 32.6
11. Field hockey — 27.9
12. Rowing/Crew — 17.4

80%   100%

TAKEN FROM: Linda Jean Carpenter and R. Vivian Acosta, "2008 Dozen Most Popular Sports All Divisions Combined," *Women in Intercollegiate Sport: A Longitudinal, National Study,* 2008.

There more than three million high school female athletes, plus all the females who participate on club and community teams, constitutes a significant pool of female athletes with ability and interest which may serve as a feeder system for college athletics programs.

Comparing NCAA Divisions

Is there a difference in participation levels between NCAA divisions? Yes. Division 1 offers the most women's teams per school with an average of 9.54. Division 3 follows next with an average of 8.78 while Division 2 trails with 7.28.

Have all NCAA divisions added teams in the last decade? Yes. Both Divisions 1 and 2 have added an average of 1.21 teams per school in the past twelve years. Division 3 has added slightly fewer with an average of 1.03.

The 1.21 and 1.03 figures are a bit misleading however. When the total number of schools offering teams for women in 2008 is considered, compared with the relatively fewer NCAA schools that offered programs for women in 1996, the average number of women's teams per school has increased by about 2.7 from 1996 to 2008 thus providing for a much fuller set of participation opportunities available nationwide for female athletes. The interest and abilities of female college athletes have not been exhausted. Many more teams are needed.

The are more than 17 times the number of varsity female high school athletes than female college athletes. Not all high school athletes attend college and not all who do attend carry with them the interest and ability to continue their athletics careers. However, common sense tells us that a significant number may be denied access to participation opportunities on the college level simply because too few opportunities for female athletes have been created even now in the face of the highest participation levels in history.

Why Are Participation Levels at Their Highest Levels Ever?

The massive increase in participation is a function of a number of factors including:

Second Generation of Title IX Beneficiaries. A generation of females has grown up in a post-Title IX era and has benefitted themselves from participating, and they expect the benefits of sport participation to be available for their daughters as well.

Lawsuits Supportive of Title IX. A long line of successful Title IX lawsuits dealing with participation and the quality of that participation has encouraged college administrators of good will to comply with the requirements of the federal law known as Title IX. *Franklin v. Gwinnett,* a key lawsuit in 1992, affirmed the availability of compensatory and punitive damages. The availability of damages has changed the financial equation considered when an institution is deciding to put more of its budget into its women's athletics program or into its legal defense/attorney budget.

Societal Acceptance of Females as Athletes. Increased participation and skill development by young women along with society's greater acceptance of female athleticism has made sport a vital part of the lives of many young women and their families.

Improved and Increased Media Coverage. Greater media time focused on female athleticism rather than solely the female form has helped young women see themselves acceptable in their own eyes, and in society, as athletes, although more needs to be done.

Advocacy Efforts of Individuals/Organizations. Successful energetic advocacy efforts have increased sport opportunities for girls and women. Among them are:

- National Association for Girls and Women in Sport

- National Association of Collegiate Women Athletic Administrators

> *"Instead, by focusing on equality of outcomes, it has made college athletics a zero sum game: women only win if men lose."*

Title IX Has Not Increased Girls' Participation in School Sports

Carrie Lukas

Carrie Lukas is a contributor to the National Review Online *and the director of policy at the* Independent Women's Forum. *The following viewpoint discusses the impact Title IX has had on colleges and universities. Lukas claims that although the law intended to provide equal opportunities for women and increase their participation in sports, ultimately in order to comply with Title IX, many men's sports teams are being cut instead.*

As you read, consider the following questions:

1. What does the author claim Title IX encourages besides female athletes' progress?

2. According to the viewpoint, what actions can universities take in order to satisfy the quota of Title IX?

Carrie Lukas, "No Gold in Gender Olympics," *National Review Online*, August 17, 2004.

3. What is the only "sure-fire" way for colleges to avoid expensive litigation?

The Super Bowl, the World Series, and March Madness all pulse with testosterone. But the Olympic Games—with heart-wrenching stories of years of sacrifice for one moment of glory in Athens—are ready-made for women. Not only do women account for more than half of the Olympics' television viewers, female athletes are Olympic stars. Networks cover women's gymnastics, diving, track, and swimming in prime-time. The Olympic Games produce superstars like Kerri Strug, whose vault clinched the U.S gymnastic team a gold medal in 1996; and Marion Jones, who sprinted to five medals in 2000.

This Olympics [2004] is no different. Among the most anticipated events is return of soccer darlings Mia Hamm and Brandi Chastain. They won the gold in 1996 and will compete one last time as a team in Athens. Swimmer Jenny Thompson already has eight gold medals to her name, and could finish her fourth Olympic Games with 13 medals.

These female Olympians deserve to be celebrated: Their hard work will inspire many young girls to participate in sports. This decision can have an important impact: Female athletes have higher graduation rates, are less likely to have unwanted pregnancies, and report higher levels of self-esteem. Sports similarly benefit boys and may play an important role in helping them socialize and form positive relationship with their peers. That's why girls and boys should both be encouraged to participate in athletic activity at early age.

The Impact of Title IX

Unfortunately, instead of just encouraging participation in sports, the federal law known as Title IX pits our male and female athletes against each other. Under this regime, it's not just female athletes' progress that's celebrated, but the elimination of male athletes.

Consider a *Washington Post* Olympic preview entitled "Female Athletes Continue to Gain Ground" written in April 2004. The article celebrated that nearly equal numbers of men and women—an estimated 282 men and 263 women—will represent the United States in Athens. It goes on to note that in the last summer Olympics, the U.S. sent 338 men and 264 women to compete.

Should these numbers really be cited as evidence of progress for women? The number of women competing was essentially unchanged. The so-called victory for women was the elimination of more than 50 male athletes from the U.S. roster.

Intention of Title IX

This mentality comes as no surprised to those familiar with the application of Title IX. This federal law was intended to prevent discrimination based on sex on college campuses, including athletics, but has since become a death sentence for many male sports teams. The only sure-fire way for colleges and universities to avoid potentially costly litigation is to make their rosters "proportional" to their enrollment. Since women account for about 56 percent of undergraduates (and there has been no outcry about the "lack of proportionality" in college enrollment) at many campuses, women need to account for *more than half* of all athletes.

To meet this quota, universities can either try to increase female participation or reduce the number of male athletes. Many have struggled to attract greater female participation. When Brown University was sued under Title IX in 1992, there were 85 unfilled spots on female varsity teams. Many universities resort to eliminating male athletic teams, including those that were once the training grounds for Olympic athletes. The University of Miami's diving program, where gold medal winner Greg Louganis received a diving scholarship, was a casualty of Title IX. Since the last Olympics, more

A Petition to the U.S. Congress for Title IX Reform

Whereas ... Today, June 23, 2008 marks the 36th anniversary of the passage of Title IX ...

Whereas ... Men's collegiate athletic teams are being eliminated and rosters are being capped at an alarming rate in order to comply with the "proportionality" enforcement prong ...

Whereas ... Women collegiate athletes are being robbed of their training partners, teammates and biggest supporters when men's teams are eliminated ...

Whereas ... Straightforward and common-sense fixes to the enforcement mechanism are already available—such as a simple survey that would allow any student, male or female, to express interest and be given opportunity ...

Whereas ... The law's current method of enforcement is discriminating against male athletes and artificially limiting opportunities to participate ...

Whereas ... The current tenor of the debate over the future of Title IX sets up a zero sum contest pitting men against women that hurts the collective cause of all college athletes ...

Be it resolved ... That men and women across the country come together to discuss and implement a set of common sense reforms to Title IX enforcement that maximizes the opportunities of all college athletes regardless of gender.

Eric McErlain,
"CSC Issues National Appeal for 'Common-Sense Reform'
to Title IX," College Sports Council, 2008. www.savingsports.org.

than ninety universities have eliminated t
men, and more than twenty have cancelled

Title IX Needs to Be Reformed

Female athletes are not celebrating the lc
Cyndi Gallagher, UCLA swimming coach, described the positive affects of having the men and women train together on
her female athletes: "When we had a men's team, we were always in the top 10." In 1994, UCLA dropped men's swimming
and diving programs, which has produced 16 Olympians.
Gallagher's conflicted feelings reveal how Title IX has drifted
away from its core mission: "I fully support Title IX. But
choosing to drop men's programs is not what Title IX wants."

Title IX was supposed to ensure that women have the opportunity to participate in athletics. Instead, by focusing on
equality of outcomes, it has made college athletics a zero sum
game: women only win if men lose. It's time for common-
sense reform to the application of Title IX that allows for
greater participation by both men and women in athletics.
That way, male and female athletes alike can come out win-
ners.

| "The all-female competitive cheer team at Maryland is fully funded and will have 12 scholarships and a $357,000 budget."

Schools Support Cheerleaders as Athletes

Jon Siegel

Jon Siegel is a reporter for the Washington Times, *a daily newspaper in the Washington, D.C., market. Siegel, in the following viewpoint, introduces the fledgling competitive cheerleading team at the University of Maryland at College Park, the first school in the United States to designate cheerleading as a scholarship sport under the terms of Title IX. The decision has drawn critics and supporters from schools nationwide. The members of the competitive cheer team do not cheer at any games, and they look forward to the day when other schools form their own varsity programs and competitive cheer gains full respect as a sport.*

As you read, consider the following questions:

1. According to Athletic Director Debbie Yow, what makes varsity cheerleading a sport?

2. According to the author, what rule prevents the University of Maryland cheerleading squad from competing at the Universal Cheerleading Association national championships?

3. Why does Kentucky cheerleading coach Jomo Thompson criticize the establishment of cheerleading as a competition-only sport, according to Siegel?

The varsity cheerleaders at the University of Maryland form pyramids like any other cheerleaders. And like any others, they flip and tumble and tirelessly practice their routines.

These cheerleaders, however, are made different by one thing they do not do: cheer at games. The squad, officially known as the competitive cheer team, performs only at cheerleading meets.

Maryland is the only university in the country that counts competitive cheer as a scholarship sport to satisfy the requirements of Title IX, the federal sex-equity law that mandates equal athletic opportunities for men and women.

The all-female competitive cheer team at Maryland is fully funded and will have 12 scholarships and a $357,000 budget when the program is completely phased in for the 2005–06 school year.

The cheerleaders who perform on the sidelines at Maryland football and basketball games are known as the "spirit squad" and do not receive scholarships.

"It's like cheerleading taken to the next level for people who take it a lot more seriously," said Mandy Shaw, a freshman from Waldorf, Md., who was recruited for a competitive cheer scholarship. "I don't like cheering at games, but I love competing."

Many schools give scholarships for cheerleading—the University of Kentucky, for example, awards 20 for tuition—but don't count them toward Title IX compliance.

Cheerleading Versus Traditional Sports

Women's groups have criticized the program at Maryland, saying the school is using cheerleading as a means to satisfy Title IX without adding an established—and likely more expensive—sport.

"It's a slippery slope," said Mary Jo Kane, the director of the Tucker Center for Research on Girls and Women in Sport at the University of Minnesota. "If they are going to set the precedent of giving scholarships to cheerleaders, why not the band? They go to competitions. They practice regularly.

"If they prioritize and say we are going to give scholarships to cheerleaders and as a result do not have enough scholarships to allow young women to have more traditional athletic opportunities, that's not OK."

Maryland administrators said they worked closely with the Department of Education's Office of Civil Rights before adding competitive cheer as a varsity sport for the 2003–04 school year.

The school was considering four women's sports for varsity status. It added competitive cheer and water polo and rejected ice hockey and rowing.

"It is a sport if you are competing," athletic director [AD] Debbie Yow said. "This is not the spirit squad. The spirit squad is busy cheering for our teams and encouraging them. The varsity cheerleading team is competing like all other sports. They are recruiting like all other sports. They are alike."

Donna Lopiano, the executive director of the Women's Sports Foundation, called the program "disingenuous." Miss Lopiano cited the team's schedule as evidence.

The Office of Civil Rights required the Terrapins [University of Maryland team] perform at eight to 10 meets each year to be considered to have held a "season" of competition for Title IX reasons. The team's Web site lists a schedule of 10 events at which the Terps [Terrapins] will perform this season [2004–2005].

However, the Terps did not compete against a Division I opponent in their first four meets this season. The team competed last month [January 2005] in the Maryland Cup, an event attended by junior high school and high school teams but no other college-level squad.

The only other college team at a meet in Baltimore was Division III Salisbury. Maryland won an open competition in December over two "all-star" club teams not affiliated with any schools.

"There is nothing wrong with that being a varsity sport as long as that is what it is," Miss Lopiano said. "It is just not developed yet, and Maryland is trying to manufacture it. The other [rejected] sports were bona fide competing entities. I don't know what was going on there. What is wrong with ice hockey? It makes a heck of a lot of sense in terms of meeting the needs of kids than not providing competition for this cheerleading group."

Terps coach Lura Fleece acknowledged that scheduling has been difficult and said the team plans to travel to more national events with more Division I teams next season.

The Obstacles to NCAA-Recognized Status

This season ends in April with the National Cheerleading Association U.S. championships in Daytona Beach, Fla., where the Terps will face about 40 all-female Division I teams. The event will be the only meet of the season for many of the Terps' opponents, who focus on cheering at games rather than at meets.

Maryland did not compete last month in what is regarded as the largest cheerleading event, the Universal Cheerleading Association (UCA) national championships. That meet requires a tape of cheerleaders performing at games.

"Our whole decision to add two sports was related to Title IX and to ensure our future Title IX compliance," said Maryland Associate Athletic Director Dave Haglund, the team's ad-

Cheerleading Is Definitely a Sport

"People have to get past the idea that cheerleading is shaking pompoms and kicking your legs in the air," said Lura Fleece, [University of] Maryland's coach, whose team completed its first official season yesterday [in April 2004] by finishing seventh in the National Cheerleading Association championships in Daytona, Florida. "Because that isn't cheerleading anymore. It's about strength and gymnastics and teamwork. We're athletes and now we compete. Just because cheerleading is all female and we're not mimicking some recognized men's sport, that means we're not a sport?" ...

"You tell some people your varsity sport is cheerleading and they roll their eyes," said Lauren Spates, a 19-year-old sophomore from St. James, New York. "That's why this step Maryland has taken is so huge. We're not just on the sidelines, we're competitors, and that earns us respect. I tell anyone who has doubts about my sport to come to a practice, and if they do that, I usually don't have to say anything more."

Bill Pennington,
"From Sideline to Stage, with Lift from Title IX,"
New York Times, *April 4, 2004.*

ministrator. "We have been accused of doing an end around Title IX. But we are really not. We are held to the same focus of other sports, where the focus is competition.

"Six, seven, eight years ago, equestrian was not an NCAA-recognized sport. It is now. Bowling is the same situation. The next step, hopefully five years or so down the line, is this becoming an NCAA-recognized sport."

The University of Kentucky has won 14 national championships in the coed division at the UCA championships. The Wildcats' coach, Jomo Thompson, doesn't like what is happening in College Park.

"What they are doing with their competition team is not cheerleading," Thompson said. "The idea of cheerleading is to build support for a team. To completely take what it was intended for and just make it competition-related, I don't agree with that. . . . I don't know the reasoning behind that—maybe so they could increase female sports participation.

"If that is the only reason they are doing it, are they really trying to legitimize the sport of cheerleading or are they just doing it for their own personal gains?"

Harold Tramel, the cheerleading coach at North Carolina State, would like sideline cheerleading to be classified as a Title IX sport.

"There's nothing wrong with what [Maryland] did," Tramel said. "It is a way to get around Title IX to be a sport. Ideally, I would like to see them change the rule. It seems too pinpointed to spite cheerleading."

Fleece, who coached the spirit squad for 11 seasons before taking over the competitive cheer team when it became a varsity sport last season, fought hard to have the sport promoted to scholarship status.

The former Maryland and [National Football League] Baltimore Ravens cheerleader said it will be a long battle before competitive cheer gains general acceptance but thinks it will happen.

Maryland's Opportunities Legitimize the Sport for Girls and Women

"It is a wonderful opportunity to provide opportunities to women," Fleece said. "The nature of the industry has really changed. All-star cheerleading [for girls] began in the mid-'90s. Little girls will only compete. All-star teams only compete. They don't cheer for any games nor do anything besides compete. This is really a natural progression. It has pushed from the ground up."

Mrs. Yow said, "We are very popular with the high school set now. They look over here at the 12 scholarships, and all those mothers and fathers and those young women are thinking, 'I am going to be recognized for all those years when people have kind of made fun of what I do.' But they have to choose not to cheer at the games."

Mrs. Yow said it was not necessary to add women's sports for Title IX reasons but that she did it to ensure that the university would be in compliance in the future. She said Maryland has more women on athletic scholarships than men for the first time and dismisses critics of competitive cheer.

"I laugh. I don't take that seriously," Mrs. Yow said. "We are so in tune with Title IX and lead in so many categories, which shouldn't be that unusual in having a female AD. It was natural for us to add water polo and this sport. . . .

"We are not on the cutting edge. [Competitive cheer] is the fourth-leading sport in high school for women. It is recognized by 22 states already as a varsity sport. [Miss Lopiano] would have been fine if we added bowling—but not this. That's why I say there is a significant degree of prejudice against cheerleading."

Mrs. Yow said sailing and equestrian were mocked when they were introduced but now are accepted as sports. She played college basketball at Elon College in North Carolina and coached at the University of Kentucky and the University of Florida. She said those experiences made her feel as if there is nothing to defend about adding the competitive cheer as a sport at Maryland.

"As a female athlete coming up through the '70s and playing collegiate ball and not having a scholarship, it is all very personal," Mrs. Yow said. "When you know what you are doing is right, at some point you just have a real peace about it and move on and let other people talk about it."

> "Cheerleading has become one of the riskiest athletic activities for women, leaving a long trail of sprained wrists, twisted ankles, damaged knees, strained backs—and sometimes much worse."

Schools Do Not Support Cheerleaders as Athletes

Rob Stein

Rob Stein is a national science reporter for the Washington Post, *focusing on health and medicine. He has been a science reporter and editor at a variety of news outlets—print and radio. In the following viewpoint, he focuses on the safety issues that plague cheerleading, a highly competitive and acrobatic activity that is not officially considered a sport. Without such a designation, high school and college squads train and operate beneath spotty safety regulations, often with improperly trained coaches. The viewpoint details some of the serious injuries and deaths that have occurred in cheerleading and compares it with other high-impact sports.*

As you read, consider the following questions:

1. Why is cheerleading considered so dangerous, according to Stein, if the actual number of catastrophic injuries is so small?

2. According to the author, why do critics believe it matters that cheerleading is considered an activity and not a sport?

3. As Jim Lord explains, when are cheerleading accidents most likely to occur?

Krista Parks was practicing with her cheerleading team when something went terribly wrong. Instead of flipping smoothly through the air and landing safely in the arms of a teammate, Parks plummeted 20 feet headfirst into the gym floor, fracturing three vertebrae in her neck.

"Immediately I went numb," said Parks, a 21-year-old University of Memphis junior at the time. "All I could feel was tingling from my head all the way down to my feet. I thought: 'I'm paralyzed.'"

Miraculously, Parks escaped permanent paralysis. But five years later, after nearly a month in the hospital, multiple surgeries, physical therapy and more, Parks has learned to live with unrelenting pain in her neck, back and head, irreparable nerve damage and memory problems.

"I'm kind of an example of the unspoken evil of what can happen in cheerleading," Parks said.

Parks's story is among the cautionary tales emerging from the increasingly popular world of cheerleading, which has evolved from prim sideline squads leading fans in the school fight song into glitzy, high-intensity, acrobatic competitive extravaganzas. Despite a sharp increase in the number and types of cheerleading squads and the complexity of their routines, cheerleading is not officially considered a sport at most high schools and universities. As a result, it's not subject to the safety regulations that apply to gymnastics, for example.

"When people think about cheerleading, they think about the girls with the pompoms jumping up and down," said Frederick O. Mueller, a leading sports injury expert at the University of North Carolina at Chapel Hill. "They don't think about someone being thrown 25 feet in the air and performing flips with twists and other risky stunts we see today."

Injuries and Fatalities

A growing body of evidence indicates cheerleading has become one of the riskiest athletic activities for women, leaving a long trail of sprained wrists, twisted ankles, damaged knees, strained backs—and sometimes much worse.

"It's getting crazy, and kids are left dying," said Ruth Burns of Malden, Massachusetts, whose 14-year-old daughter Ashley Marie died in 2005 after her spleen ruptured when she landed stomach-down following an airborne spin while practicing with her high school cheerleading squad. "Most parents have no idea. They just assume that it's safe."

The most recent catastrophe occurred in April [2008], when Lauren Chang, 20, of Newton, Massachusetts, died after apparently getting kicked in the chest during a cheerleading competition involving a team she had joined at a local gym.

"I think it's a crisis—a national crisis," said Kimberly Archie, executive director and founder of the National Cheer Safety Foundation, a private nonprofit group in Irvine, California, trying to publicize cases like Parks's. "It's kind of flown under the radar."

While cheerleading proponents acknowledge that more could be done to improve safety, they dispute claims that the activity is unusually risky.

"When it's done properly, cheerleading is as safe as any other sport that kids can take part in," said Jim Lord, executive director of the American Association of Cheerleading Coaches and Administrators. "I don't want to minimize the fact that there are risks, and injuries can occur. I just think it has to be put into perspective."

As Safe as Any Other Sport?

Concerns about cheerleading safety arise whenever a high-profile accident occurs. But alarm spiked again this summer when the National Center for Catastrophic Sports Injury Research, which has been tracking sports safety nationwide for 25 years, reported that cheerleading accounted for two-thirds of all catastrophic injuries among female high school and college athletes.

The total number of "catastrophic" incidents, defined as death or serious injury, such as head or neck damage leading to permanent disability, was relatively small. The center documented just 93 such cases between 1982 and 2007: 67 that occurred among high school students and 26 in college. And although other sports, such as football, produce far more devastating injuries, Mueller, who runs the center, calculated that the numbers translate into a rate of 2.68 catastrophic injuries for every 100,000 female high school cheerleaders, which exceeds the rate for many other high school sports.

"This tells you that cheerleading is dangerous—even more dangerous than football when it comes to the rate," said Mueller, noting that because there is no reporting system for cheerleading accidents, the problem is probably worse. "I think it's a serious problem, and it has to be looked at. I think cheerleading has to make some dramatic changes."

Lord and others, however, challenge Mueller's estimate, saying they are based on an underestimate of cheerleading participation by at least half, making the catastrophic accident rate appear far higher than it really is.

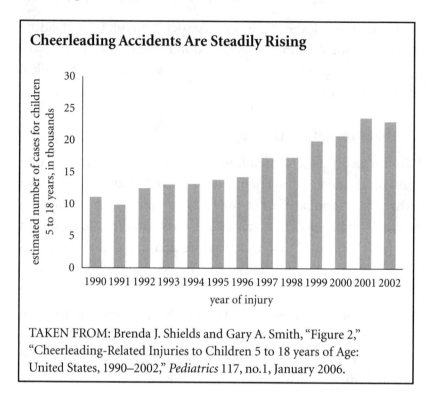

Cheerleading Accidents Are Steadily Rising

TAKEN FROM: Brenda J. Shields and Gary A. Smith, "Figure 2,"
"Cheerleading-Related Injuries to Children 5 to 18 years of Age:
United States, 1990–2002," *Pediatrics* 117, no.1, January 2006.

"His numbers are skewed," said Susan Loomis, cheerleading director for the National Federation of State High School
Associations. "Cheerleading has become much, much safer in
the last 15 or 20 years."

Other research indicates the overall injury toll from cheerleading has been rising sharply. Based on emergency room
data from 114 hospitals, the Consumer Product Safety Com-
mission estimated that the number of emergency room visits
to treat cheerleading injuries of any kind jumped from 4,954
in 1980 to 28,414 in 2004. Similarly, a study published in the
journal *Pediatrics* in 2006 calculated that the number of children showing up in emergency rooms with cheerleading injuries rose from 10,900 in 1990 to 22,900 in 2002, a 110 percent
increase.

The most common injuries were arm and leg strains and
sprains, but 3.5 percent of the cases involved head injuries.

Cheerleading "has the potential to be very dangerous," said Brenda J. Shields, who runs the Center for Injury Research and Policy at Nationwide Children's Hospital in Columbus, Ohio, and led the *Pediatrics* study.

Although Shields said she also thought Mueller overestimated the rate of catastrophic accidents, her tally did not include many more minor injuries that never make it to the hospital.

"They are treated by coaches, trainers and private doctors," Shields said.

No Standards for Training or Safety

The main problem, critics say, is that cheerleading in most states is not considered a sport; it's an "activity" such as chess club and debating. As a result, it is not required to follow uniform safety regulations, such as mandating off-seasons, routine physicals and soft surfaces that would minimize injuries. Coaches are not required to undergo standardized training.

In addition to thousands of junior high, high school and college squads fulfilling their traditional role of cheering on football, basketball and other teams, competitive cheerleading teams, many organized by private gyms and some of them fighting for prize money, have been proliferating across the country, increasing the number of participants sharply. The intensifying competition has been pushing teams to attempt increasingly complex stunts.

"One set of rules and regulations doesn't apply to all the different teams that are out there," Shields said.

Lord's and Loomis's organizations issue safety guidelines that are updated annually. For example, this year's rules recommend against "basket tosses" (in which multiple teammates throw a cheerleader spinning into the air) on a hard basketball court floor.

Cheerleading "should be treated like other sports in terms of having a qualified coach and following safety rules to put children in a safe position," Lord said. "It comes down to following those rules."

Several organizations also offer training programs for coaches, including how to minimize risks, teach stunts properly and respond to medical emergencies.

"Our mind-set is still set in the '70s. People think of the girls in short little skirts waving pompoms. But they are finely honed athletes. We need to make sure they are getting the coaching that will keep them safe and keep that coaching on an elevated level," said Debbie Bracewell, executive director of the National Council of Spirit Safety and Education, which along with Loomis's and Lord's groups offers training programs for coaches.

But Archie and other critics say the rules and training are inadequate. And because they are voluntary, their application varies widely across the country. "It's a hodgepodge, and even where they say they follow the rules, there's no one really enforcing that," Archie said.

Improving the Coaches

Lord acknowledged that the rules and the training of coaches vary significantly and that some teams are attempting dangerous stunts without adequate preparation and safeguards.

"We're seeing more kids trying skills they shouldn't try. That's where the injuries occur. When we see that and see an increase in injuries, we make a rule change and say regardless of what your team can do we're not going to allow it," Lord said. "I want to make sure we have qualified coaches in place. We also need parents to be involved to make sure they are following the rules. And the kids who participate have to recognize there is risk involved."

Part of the problem, Bracewell said, is schools do not do a good enough job making sure they hire qualified coaches and pay to keep their training up to date.

"If schools would hire cheerleading coaches as vigorously as they hire football and basketball coaches, you'd see a difference in those statistics," she said.

Loomis predicts safety will continue to improve.

"We're the new kid on the block, and as we improve safety and teaching of our coaches we'll see fewer and fewer injuries," Loomis said. "We may have a long way to go, but we're certainly getting better. There is a risk in any athletic activity."

For her part, Parks, who now works as physical therapist, says she hopes more attention will lead to better safety for other cheerleaders.

"My whole life was just taken out from under me," Parks said. "These accidents happen way more than they should. I'm just hoping that something finally gets done about it."

Periodical Bibliography

The following articles have been selected to supplement the diverse views presented in this chapter.

Anne Delaney   "Gender Equity Prompted Girls Pairings Telecast," *Utica Observer-Dispatch (New York)*, April 5, 2009.

Sara Foss   "Girls in Game, but Score Not Yet Tied," *Schenectady Daily Gazette (New York)*, September 23, 2007.

Jesus M. Gandara   "Sweetwater Union Pushing for Gender Equity in Sports," *San Diego Union Tribune*, April 11, 2009.

Hannah Hoffman   "Students Donate Training, Gear to Kenyan Orphanage," *Oregon Daily Emerald (University of Oregon)*, May 7, 2009.

Winnie Hu   "Equal Cheers for Boys and Girls Draws Some Boos," *New York Times*, January 14, 2007.

Sara Lipka and Brad Wolverton   "Title IX Enforcement Called 'Deeply Troubling,'" *Chronicle of Higher Education*, June 29, 2007.

David Murphy   "Gender Bias a Concern in Prep Steroid Testing," *St. Petersburg Times*, June 17, 2007.

Connie Paige   "Gender's Role in Fair Play," *Boston Globe*, May 17, 2009.

Thomas J. Ryan   "Women's Sports Face New Challenges: Cutback in School Programs and the Rise of Youth Leagues Are the Latest Hurdles," *Sporting Goods Business*, March 2008.

Jane M. Shimon   "Activity Choice and Title IX," *Journal of Physical Education, Recreation, and Dance*, November/December 2007.

OPPOSING
VIEWPOINTS®
SERIES

CHAPTER 4

What Are the Cultural Implications of Girls' Participation in Sports?

Chapter Preface

In the 1880s and 1890s, the world went mad for bicycles. Faster than walking and much cheaper to own and care for than a horse, a bicycle expanded the range of its owner's personal mobility, enabling riders to travel faster and see more of the world. Women were not immune to the joys of bicycling and flocked to the pastime in droves—to the consternation of religious leaders, physicians, and social critics alike. Objections to cycling for women ranged from concerns about the negative effects of the activity on women's moral behavior and their ability to bear children to the worry that they would spend so much time outdoors that men would be left with the housework and end up as the subjugated sex.

In fact, some historians have argued the invention of the bicycle has done more to elevate the social and political status of women than any other technology or phenomenon. Bicycling improved women's health with exercise and prompted a change in clothing styles: heavy, long skirts and chest-constricting corsets gave way to looser, shorter dresses and even "bloomers"—a draping, gathered trouser that would not catch in a bicycle's gears or chains. In an 1896 interview with *New York World* journalist Nellie Bly, suffragist icon Susan B. Anthony proclaimed that bicycling "has done more to emancipate woman than any one thing in the world. I rejoice every time I see a woman ride by on a wheel. It gives her a feeling of self-reliance and independence the moment she takes her seat." Women formed cycling groups and participated in long-distance events, getting a taste of equality to men on the cycling paths and developing the confidence and sense of independence that would carry them through to the success of the suffrage movement in the early twentieth century.

More than a century later, the idea that sports can change the lives of girls and women as a group has not lost its relevance. Many programs worldwide reach out to girls—especially girls in patriarchal or restrictive societies—to teach them the passion for and skills to play sports to give them confidence and promote gender equity. For example, the stated objectives of the Association of Kigali Women in Sports include helping Rwandan women promote their rights and self-confidence, promote awareness about the HIV/AIDS pandemic, create a forum for ethnic and religious integration and reconciliation, and provide a meeting point between elite and impoverished women so they can exchange ideas. World champion boxer Tareq Shawl Azim trains girls and women in Afghanistan to box as a way to help reform and restore pride in that war-torn nation. Wherever girls grow up playing sports, they identify and develop their abilities and power and learn how to cooperate with each other to achieve shared goals. These skills are easily transferred to coping with adult challenges, whether on the scale of increasing personal income or being able to stay healthy, or on the scale of rewriting national policy or changing cultural traditions to improve the lives of women as a group.

That sports participation can change women's lives for the better is acknowledged even in wealthy, stable nations such as the United States. A 2002 report published by the Mass Mutual Financial Group, *From the Locker Room to the Board Room*, reveals that 82 percent of American executive businesswomen played sports as girls and attribute their career success directly to lessons learned on the field and in training. Even at the level of casual play, a girl who participates in sports regularly is more likely to stand up for herself. Sports have always been known to have this effect on boys and men; giving girls today the same athletic opportunities as male peers gives women of future generations the same social and political power.

The following chapter addresses some of the social changes that have come about since girls started participating in sports and how these changes have benefited or harmed women as individuals or in general.

> *"At least one-third of collegiate cross-country runners suffer from some sort of eating disorder."*

Female Endurance Athletes Diet to Improve Performance

Eli Saslow

Currently a staff writer for the national news at the Washington Post, *Eli Saslow spent several years writing for its sports section; the following viewpoint dates from that period. He shows a decline in girls' participation in cross-country running as they advance through high school. Although freshman and sophomore runners are very fast distance runners, the changes in their weight, stance, and body fat as they mature diminish their performance ability. Training cannot overcome biology. As a result, some girls abandon the sport, but others develop eating disorders to keep their weight low for short-term gains and long-term damage.*

As you read, consider the following questions:

1. As Saslow explains, how does the natural weight gain of a maturing female body affect adolescent runners?

Eli Saslow, "In Prep Cross-Country, Girls Often Face an Uphill Battle," *The Washington Post*, September 16, 2006, p. A01. Copyright © 2006 *The Washington Post*. Reprinted with permission.

2. According to coach Ed Purpura, why do so many girls abandon the cross-country team in high school?

3. What are the negative effects of eating disorders on the female body as the author details?

Kay Comer sometimes felt stuck in a stranger's body. She looked in the mirror last summer [2006] and saw few remnants of the scrawny high school freshman whom cross-country coaches had once referred to as "lungs with legs." Comer's hips had expanded. Her shoulders had broadened. Her thighs had developed more muscle.

Only a year earlier, Comer won a district championship at Colonial Forge High School in Stafford [Va.] and earned a reputation as Virginia's up-and-coming distance runner. Now, even her shortest jogs ended in a hobbled limp.

"I went through a stage where running was hard and it hurt everywhere," Comer said. "I just didn't want to do it."

Like most female cross-country runners, Comer has faced much greater hardship than the typical high school athlete who grows up, builds muscle and improves each season. In girls' cross-country, runners are more likely to regress than progress. Forty high school sophomores earned All-Met honors—either first team, second team or honorable mention—between 2000 and 2003. Only 15 of those girls, or 38 percent, earned an equal or better distinction as seniors.

Unfortunate Timing for a Biological Change

Coaches, doctors, and athletes blame that decline on a degenerative cycle that threatens many young female athletes, particularly distance runners. Physiological changes during puberty temporarily make running less natural, and rebelling against those changes results in injuries and eating disorders. The ailing athlete then loses confidence and, ultimately, interest in the sport.

"It's kind of heartbreaking for the girls to realize that they can try as hard as ever and the performance still isn't there," said Severna Park [Md.] cross-country coach Ed Purpura, whose girls' team won the 2005 Maryland 3A title. "It's always the elephant in the room in our sport. Nobody likes to talk about it, but everybody knows that's often how it works."

College and high school coaches estimate that about 80 percent of female runners will level off, at least temporarily, because of physiological changes. The average girl gains about 10 or 20 pounds during high school, doctors said, and much of the added weight consists of natural fat. Nutritionists suggest women must maintain at least 17 percent body fat to menstruate; top male athletes, meanwhile, often thrive on less than 10 percent.

For female runners, that extra weight can create uncomfortable pressure on knees, ankles and shins during high-impact activities. That discomfort is compounded by widened hips, which can change a runner's stride and add to the stress on her knees.

In the early 1990s, the University of Washington studied 60,000 teenage athletes and concluded that girls' cross-country had the highest injury rate of any sport, with more than 60 injuries for every 100 runners each season. Typically, women become strong runners again early in college, coaches said, when tendons and muscles adjust to the added weight and compensate for the altered stride.

Female Runners Are Particularly Vulnerable

All female athletes must adjust to these body changes, doctors said. But the transition is hardest in cross-country, diving, gymnastics and ice skating—activities where small size often is considered advantageous.

Comer, now a junior at Colonial Forge, remains an elite runner, but even the best athletes hardly are immune to the trend—start fast and finish slower—that defines girls' cross-

Eating Disorders Are More Prevalent Among College Athletes

Collegiate athletes displayed higher levels of disordered eating, body dissatisfaction, and excessive exercise than did high school athletes. When a high school athlete moves to collegiate-level competition, it is generally believed to be a positive step forward, and rarely are the negative side effects considered. However, previous studies have found that the levels of stress placed on collegiate athletes tend to be much greater than those placed on high school athletes. As a result, the added pressure placed on athletes to perform at a collegiate level may cause athletes to put their health at risk by engaging in behaviors such as disordered eating and excessive exercise. This may be in part because coaches tend to favor athletes who excessively exercise or favor leaner body types. In addition, in the name of 'sport ethic' athletes may put pressures on themselves at the expense of their health. These unhealthy behaviors may also be due to an athlete's inability to reach his or her perceived ideal, generally leaner, body type, which could then lead to body dissatisfaction and ultimately the unhealthy behaviors of disordered eating and excessive exercise.

Mary Pritchard, Paul Rush, and BreeAnn Milligan,
"Risk Factors for Disordered Eating in
High School and College Athletes," Athletic Insight:
The Online Journal of Sport Psychology, *2007.*

country. While male runners gain height and muscle mass during puberty and quickly lower their times, girls struggle to maintain early success.

Marissa McPhail, a freshman on a running scholarship at Fresno State [California State University at Fresno], said she still hasn't been able to equal the times she ran as a 14-year-old freshman at Arundel High School [Gambrills, Md.]. Comer's times slowed between her freshman and sophomore years. "It's kind of like you just had to start running in winter clothes," she said.

"It rocks to be that freshman who is up there with the seniors, but you know you're not going to see those same jumps of success later in your career," said Stefanie Slekis, a 2006 graduate of Forest Park High School in Woodbridge [Va.]. "If you start that fast, sometimes you're just trying to hang on."

Slekis said running felt almost effortless when she was a high school freshman and sophomore. She weighed only about 105 pounds, and 3.1-mile cross-country races rarely tired her. Now, as a freshman on the cross-country team at Syracuse University [N.Y.], Slekis competes at about 130 pounds.

"I'm a stronger athlete, but that was kind of a big transition in terms of running," said Slekis, who adjusted to her natural weight gain and became an All-Met as a junior and senior. "When I was a freshman, I was practically frail. But I could definitely run fast."

Coaches and doctors said that young, lean girls possess running advantages. Narrow hips allow a girl's legs to hit the ground at a 90-degree angle, reducing the strain on ankles and knees. Lighter athletes tend to use oxygen more efficiently, so they rarely run out of breath.

Purpura guided Severna Park to the state championship last year [2005] with a varsity team that comprised four freshmen, two sophomores and a senior. The coach sent his runners into the offseason with candid advice. "Next year's freshmen are going to be just as good," Purpura said. "You're going to have to work harder to stay where you are."

Training Cannot Overcome Biology

But too often, hard work is futile. In the last five years, Severna Park has had two all-state sophomore runners who failed to make the varsity team as seniors. Purpura said many of his juniors and seniors give up cross-country because they feel frustrated and powerless against regression. This season, 51 girls came out for Purpura's team. Only three were seniors.

"When it's not working out, they vote with their legs and walk away," Purpura said. "They say, 'I don't want to do this anymore.' They find other things they're good at or try something new, and who can blame them?"

Said Alison Smith, a senior at Atholton High in Columbia [Md.] and the two-time defending Maryland 2A champion: "You get heavier and you hit a plateau where you stop improving. You lose focus and things pile up. It's like, 'How can I ever fix this?'"

The only answer, coaches said, usually strikes runners as counterintuitive: do nothing. Fighting maturation is pointless, coaches said, and it can lead to consequences much more severe than disappointing race results.

Katherine Beals ran on the cross-country team at the University of California-Davis more than 20 years ago, and her coaches instituted a strict policy against weight gain. Beals and her teammates sometimes weighed in before practices, and coaches stood in front of the team and asked certain runners to lose weight. As a result, Beals said, at least four or five runners suffered from anorexia and bulimia.

Beals has devoted her career to helping athletes prevent such things from happening. She wrote a book on athletes with eating disorders. She became a nutrition professor at the University of Utah, where she screens incoming athletes for dangerous eating habits. Beals estimates that at least one-third of collegiate cross-country runners suffer from some sort of eating disorder. Other college coaches guessed that number could be closer to 50 percent at Division I schools.

"It's so common that some coaches almost accept it as part of the sport," Beals said. "With cross-country, sometimes there's actually a reason to be thinner, since you have to transport that weight through space. That creates a dangerous temptation."

How Eating Disorders Affect Performance

An eating disorder typically helps an athlete improve as a runner for about six months, doctors and coaches said. Then the consequences are inevitable and disastrous. An eating disorder often leads to amenorrhea, the absence of menstruation. Amenorrhea decreases bone density. Low bone density leads to stress fractures and osteoporosis.

It's a cause and effect that every cross-country coach knows well—"the downfall of our sport," Georgetown University [Washington, D.C.] Coach Ron Helmer said—but even experts struggle to address it. Regression, injuries, and eating disorders make for uncomfortable conversations, and some high school coaches said they hardly feel comfortable confronting young runners with such negativity. Other coaches, though, said full disclosure works as the best preventative measure.

Almost all cross-country summer camps include seminars on nutrition. Local club coach Brian Funk said he asks every girl he coaches about her menstrual cycle. Sometimes the conversations feel awkward, Funk said, but they allow him to gauge an athlete's sustenance.

"You can't shy away from a tough topic in this sport, because bad things will happen," said Mike Mangan, coach at Lake Braddock Secondary School in Burke [Va.]. "If a girl's body is changing, I'm going to be honest from the start. I'm not going to tell them: 'Hey, don't worry about it. You'll be fine in a few weeks.' I'm going to be upfront. I'm going to tell them: 'We're in for a long road, but we're going to try work through it. You can be a stronger runner and a better person on the other side.'"

"Gymnasts realize they look good and thin enough in daily life, but believe they need a thinner body for their sport to enhance their physical ability."

Female Aesthetic Athletes Diet to Improve Performance

A.P. (Karin) de Bruin, Raoul R.D. Oudejans, and Frank C. Bakker

A.P. (Karin) de Bruin, Raoul R.D. Oudejans, and Frank C. Bakker are members of the faculty of human movement sciences at Vrije University in Amsterdam, Netherlands. In the following viewpoint, they investigate the prevalence of eating disorders among elite competitive gymnasts and the motivations for excessive dieting. Research shows that elite athletes do not generally have a negative body image, which is the cause of many eating disorders among regular girls. Rather, athletes competing at elite levels diet because they believe a smaller body will help them win more events and because they believe coaches and trainers want them to do so.

A.P. (Karin) de Bruin, Raoul R.D. Oudejans, and Frank C. Bakker, "Dieting and Body Image in Aesthetic Sports," *Psychology of Sport and Exercise*, vol. 8, July 2007, pp. 507–20. Copyright © 2007 Elsevier B.V. All rights reserved. Reproduced with permission from Elsevier, conveyed through Copyright Clearance Center, Inc.

As you read, consider the following questions:

1. Because athletes are generally satisfied with their body images, what reasons have been given by the authors to explain why they diet excessively?

2. According to the researchers, what belief correlates to the frequency of dieting among nonelite athletes?

3. What quality do nonathletes often associate with being thin, according to the study?

There is quite some evidence that female athletes are at increased risk of developing eating disorders, particularly when they are performing at the elite level. Because athletes often do not meet the exact criteria for clinical eating disorders, so-called sub-clinical eating disorders appear to be more common among them. Some authors even introduced 'anorexia athletica', a sub-clinical eating disorder with sport-specific diagnostic criteria, or prefer to talk about the broader concept of disordered eating in this context.

The prevalence of eating disorder symptomatology seems to be different in various sports with significantly more symptoms in athletes in aesthetic, endurance, and weight-dependent sports than in technical sports, ball games, and power sports, or in non-athletes. Problems are mainly found in sports that emphasize leanness, thinness, and aesthetic aspects, such as gymnastics, dance, figure skating, synchronized swimming, and diving. Particularly young gymnasts are often pointed out as the athletes most at risk. Pathogenic weight control was used most frequently by gymnasts in comparison to other athletes. [Lionel W.] Rosen and [David O.] Hough found that 62% of the female college gymnasts in their sample used at least one method of pathogenic weight control, such as fasting, self-induced vomiting, or using laxatives, diuretics, or diet pills. However, in a recent meta-analysis [combining the results of several reports] of eating problems in female athletes, elite gymnasts competing successfully at national or international levels or as professional competitors did not significantly differ from non-athletes.

Besides research on prevalence there are also a growing number of studies trying to detect so-called risk factors for developing eating disorders. A variety of risk-factor models for eating disorders have been proposed, including multiple putative individual, family, and socio-cultural risk factors. Factors like body image dissatisfaction, weight concerns and actual dieting behavior are nearly always part of these models, and a negative body image is found to be a very potent, well-supported risk factor. Individuals with a negative body image often worry about their weight, are afraid to gain weight and therefore diet more often than persons who have less weight concerns.

The Relationship Between Body Image and Eating Disorders

In general, body image refers to "the mental image a person has of his or her physical appearance, as well as any positive or negative feelings one has about his or her body shape or size" and should be considered a multi-dimensional concept, in which actual body characteristics as well as perceived, ideal and social body images can be distinguished.

There is increasing evidence that body image disturbances often precede eating disorders. Two components of disturbance have been distinguished, namely perceptual body-size distortion and a negative attitudinal or affective element. "Perceptual distortion consists of inaccurate judgments of one's body size. The attitudinal component consists of dissatisfaction with one's body size, shape or some other aspect of body appearance." Both can serve as independent measures to predict eating disorders, although attitudinal measures have more clinical relevance and yield more consistent findings. Among athletes attitudinal body image disturbances also appeared to contribute to patterns of disordered eating and dieting.

Because of the presumably higher prevalence of disordered eating in athletes in weight-related sport types and the alleged presence of attitudinal body image disturbances in all individuals with eating disorder symptomatology, a more negative body image among these athletes might be expected. However, a recent meta-analytic review of 78 studies examining the general body image of athletes concluded that athletes have a slightly more positive body image than non-athletes. No differences were found among athletes in aesthetic, endurance, and ball game sport types, indicating that even the aesthetic athletes who are most at risk for developing eating disorders, had a more positive body image and were more satisfied with their body.

[Linda] Smolak et al. proposed that disordered eating in athletes might differ from that in non-athletes after finding an atypical combination of a high drive for thinness and a low rather than a high score on body dissatisfaction in athletes. Similarly, [Paula J.] Ziegler et al. showed that junior elite figure skaters dieted despite being relatively satisfied with their body. In both studies, the athletes' desire for thinness or actual dieting did not appear to be associated with body dissatisfaction. Alternatively, it has been suggested that in weight-related sport types, it is especially the athletes' assumption that success is associated with low body weight or fat content, that might lead to weight concerns and subsequent attempts to reduce weight, either gradually (e.g., by dieting or exercising) or rapidly (e.g., by vomiting). Other studies pointed to weight-related pressures of the coach as a general explanation for the high prevalence of disordered eating in athletes. In sum, the results of Smolak et al. and Ziegler et al. dispute common ideas in athletes of dieting being linked to body dissatisfaction. Instead of the 'negative body image explanation', relationships with weight-related causal attributions or coach pressure have been posited as alternative explanations for dieting behavior and disordered eating in athletes. . . .

Predictions About Gymnasts' Body Images and Eating Behaviors

First, it was hypothesized that gymnasts, specifically the elites, would demonstrate more symptoms related to disordered eating than the controls. More specifically, we expected a larger desire for weight loss of the gymnasts, particularly the elites. We also expected the gymnasts, particularly the elites, to show more frequent dieting and pathogenic weight control than controls [non-aesthetic athletes].

Regarding body image, it was expected that gymnasts would be equally satisfied with their body or even have a more positive body image than controls. Nonetheless, it was uncertain whether this would apply to every dimension, i.e., perceived body shape [too thin–too fat], perceived body size [too small–too large], perceived body appearance [ugly–beautiful] and perceived opinion of others about one's body [negative–positive].

With respect to the relationships between dieting and body image, it was hypothesized that, in line with common ideas, the dieting behavior of controls would be related to a more negative body image. More specifically, we expected that frequent dieting would be related to a higher BMI [body mass index value], to a larger desire to lose weight, to a more negative (read: more fat) perceived body shape, as well as to a more negative (read: less beautiful) perceived appearance. The dimension perceived body size seemed to be less relevant for dieting and was put aside.

Furthermore, among controls we expected the weight characteristics and perceived body shape to be negatively correlated with perceived body appearance. This would indicate that the lower their BMI or the thinner their perceived shape, the more controls would perceive their body appearance as beautiful, corresponding with the common idea that 'thin is beautiful'.

Among gymnasts, we expected to find significant relationships between frequent dieting on the one hand and a higher BMI, and a more fat perceived body shape on the other hand, as these results have been found earlier. However, no relationships were expected between dieting and perceived body appearance (ugly–beautiful dimension). Furthermore, if dieting is indeed related to weight and shape, but not to appearance, perhaps weight and shape will not be significantly correlated with appearance either, which would indicate that the idea that 'thin is beautiful' will not apply to gymnasts. Alternatively, for the gymnasts' dieting we expected positive correlations with weight-related causal attributions of success and failure, as well as with the perceived weight-related pressure of the coach, which would indicate that their dieting behavior fits better with the idea that 'thin is going to win'. . . .

How Do Athletes Compare to Nonathletes?

Furthermore, among the controls we expected the body weight characteristics (BMI and relative weight discrepancy) and perceived body shape to be significantly correlated to perceived body appearance, in contrast to the gymnasts. Results showed that the perceived body appearance of the controls was moderately related to BMI and strongly to perceived body shape. The lower their actual body weight, or the thinner their perceived shape, the more beautiful controls perceived their body appearance. The moderate positive relationship between perceived appearance and relative weight discrepancy indicated that controls who wanted to gain weight, perceived their body as more beautiful, while the girls who desired weight loss perceived their body as less beautiful.

For elites and non-elites, correlations between perceived body appearance and BMI, perceived shape, or relative weight discrepancy were not significant and weak, except for a non-significant moderate relationship between perceived shape and appearance in elites. A strong positive correlation was found between the gymnasts' dieting and perceived weight-related coach pressure for elites, and a moderate positive correlation was found for non-elites. The gymnasts' dieting frequency is higher when the perceived weight-related pressure of their coach is higher. For non-elites, a moderate positive correlation was also found between dieting and weight-related causal attributions of failure, as well as a moderate positive relationship with weight-related causal attributions of success. The stronger their own belief in that failure is caused by (alleged) overweight or that success is related to weight, shape and appearance, the more frequently non-elites dieted.

The main purpose of the present study was to investigate the relationships among dieting behaviors and the multidimensional body image in gymnasts and 'average' schoolgirls. We hypothesized that gymnasts, particularly elites, would show more symptoms related to disordered eating. Even though gymnasts showed a significantly lower BMI than the controls, they seemed to desire weight loss at least as much as the controls did. After controlling for BMI, both elites and non-elites showed a significantly larger relative weight discrepancy. Bearing in mind that due to their greater lean-muscle mass athletes are in fact thinner than their BMI indicates, the gymnasts' desire for weight loss should be considered as extra unhealthy. Moreover, elites dieted more frequently than controls, and seemed to have used pathogenic dieting such as self-induced vomiting more often, especially when 'weight-related exercise' which is probably a healthier method to lose weight in controls, was put aside. . . .

Regarding body image, we assumed that gymnasts would have an equal or slightly more positive body image. Elites had higher scores than controls on all body image dimensions but none of the differences reached the significance level; therefore

A Coach and a Former Athlete Reflect on Eating Disorders

Coach: There seem to be a number of factors that cause eating disorders. I have found that athletes with very intense type A personalities are at risk. This type of personality coupled with being in an aesthetic judged sport can often lead to disordered eating. Quite often, the athletes have an overweight mother or sister. Their desire "not to be like mom" can contribute to the development of an eating disorder. Sometimes when an athlete has gone through a difficult emotional experience, an eating disorder can develop. This is usually a cry for attention or help. The culture of the sport can contribute to the development of an eating disorder. For example, if younger athletes have role models who have disordered eating, there is a higher probability that the younger athletes will adopt similar behaviors.

Athlete: When I look back on my teen years, there were signs that I was susceptible to an eating disorder. The summer I first qualified for the national team, the team sport psychologist conducted a profile of me, which I found while cleaning out my parents' attic. The profile measured my self-esteem as a swimmer and as a person, as well as a variety of other factors such as precompetition nerves. The sport psychologist noted that my self-esteem as a swimmer was off the charts, whereas my self-esteem as a person was extremely low, and he pointed out that it could be a problem if I continued to see myself as only a swimmer and did not improve my view of myself as a person.

Jim Taylor and Gregory Scott Wilson, eds., Applying Sport Psychology: Four Perspectives, *Human Kinetics, 2005, p. 217.*

the conclusion seems justified that their body image is at the least equal to that of the controls. Non-elites appeared to be significantly more positive about their perceived appearance as well as about the perceived opinions of other girls and boys. Overall, these findings are in accordance with the meta-analysis of [Heather A.] Hausenblas and [Danielle] Symons Downs, revealing a more positive body image in athletes, narrowing it down to the dimension 'body appearance'.

Putting these results together, elites reported more actual dieting and weight control, in spite of the fact that they were not more dissatisfied with their bodies. These results are consistent with the findings of Smolak et al. and Ziegler et al., who disputed that disordered eating and frequent dieting in athletes are linked to body image dissatisfaction. The finding that both elite and non-elite gymnasts reported a larger relative weight discrepancy than controls without being more dissatisfied with their body could also be taken as support for [Rob] Sands' conclusion that a drive for thinness is perhaps not as closely related to the concept of body image as is often assumed.

Why Athletes Diet

In the present study we distinguished multiple body image components and found that dieting behavior of gymnasts was related differently to their body image than the dieting of the controls. Among gymnasts dieting was notably related to actual (BMI) and perceived body shape. Among controls, additional significant relationships of medium strength were found between dieting and perceived body appearance as well as with the perceived opinion of other girls. Moreover, among controls the dimensions weight and shape were strongly correlated with appearance: The lower their BMI and thinner their perceived shape, the more positive and beautiful controls perceived their body, leading to the conclusion that the average schoolgirl seems to believe that 'thin is beautiful'. The corresponding correlations were not significant and weaker for the gymnasts, suggesting that this 'thin is beautiful' explanation may be less applicable to them. . . .

When the focus is directed at the amount of shared variance, it becomes apparent that 16.6% of the elites' dieting seems to be explained by perceived appearance compared to 18.5% of the controls' dieting. However, no less than 64% of the variance of the elites' dieting was explained by weight-related coach pressure. Also in non-elites, sport-specific variables such as causal attributions for failure (24%) and success (13%), as well as coach pressure (10%) seemed to explain more variance of their dieting behavior than perceived appearance (6%). It would be good to confirm these relationships in future studies with larger samples and for instance with other athletes such as males or sport participants in other sports. In addition, the influence of other sport-specific factors, such as motivational climate, goal perspective, perceived competence and body image in and outside the sport arena should be investigated.

With respect to the current study, perhaps gymnasts realize they look good and thin enough in daily life, but believe they need a thinner body for their sport to enhance their physical ability. This idea would fit the multidimensional approach that considers physical appearance and physical ability as separate constructs and refers to the notion of transient body satisfaction 'on and off the pitch'. Indeed, significant correlations were found between the gymnasts' dieting and weight-related causal attributions of success and failure and perceived weight-related coach pressure. The stronger their own belief or that of their coach that failure is caused by their (alleged) overweight, the more frequently gymnasts diet. It seems that gymnasts are rather convinced or persuaded that 'thin is going to win'.

> *"As girls participate more in competitive athletic activities, . . . they will become more likely to resort to aggression when they become aroused by anger or frustration."*

Sports Participation Increases Aggression in Females

James Garbarino

James Garbarino holds the Maude C. Clarke chair in humanistic psychology at Loyola University in Chicago and is a fellow of the American Psychological Association; he has served as consultant or adviser to a wide range of organizations, including the National Institute for Mental Health. The following excerpt is from his book, See Jane Hit, *an explanation for why girls have become more aggressive as a group. He attributes part of it to their participation in sports, although he blames adults—parents, coaches, members of the media—for letting this aggression become a socially toxic expression of female physicality.*

As you read, consider the following questions:

1. What positive outcomes does the author associate with girls playing sports in high school?

2. According to neurobiologist Kassandra Christiansen, how does playing competitive sports affect the body's release of testosterone?

3. What external factors does Garbarino list that are affecting the increase of hostile aggression in children's sports?

Participation of teenage girls in competitive athletics and recreational sports has risen dramatically in recent decades, offering physical and psychological benefits that include the girls' seeing their physical power in domains beyond sexuality. But these experiences can also validate physical aggression in girls.

When I was in high school in the 1960s, boys played on the athletic teams; girls cheered them on. Very few girls played sports, and only a handful of boys cheered. This has changed dramatically; at least the girls playing sports part has. . . . According to the National Federation of State High School Associations, in 1970 one in twenty-seven high school girls played a varsity sport. By 2002 it was one in three! In 1970, for every girl who played a varsity sport in high school there were thirty-five boys, a ratio of 35:1. In 2002 there were nearly three million girls playing varsity sports in high school and nearly four million boys. That means the ratio of girls to boys was 1:1.33. Now that's social and cultural change.

Sports Promote Positive Physicality in Girls

What does this mean for girls? It undoubtedly means that girls who would have been drawn to sports in an earlier era but who might have forgone the opportunity because of fear of being labeled negatively can now join teams without fear-ing that their participation in sports will compromise their femininity. What would have been a tomboy then is now just a girl who likes sports. In the bad old days tomboys were at best tolerated; in the new era girl athletes are celebrated.

It's hard to say with certainty what the overall effects of this on girls are, however. Because participation is mostly voluntary, you can't be sure that any differences you observe between athletic girls and nonathletic girls are due to their participation in sports or the reason behind that participation in the first place. Nonetheless, studies do at least document that playing sports in high school is associated with certain positive outcomes for girls. These include being 92 percent less likely to use drugs compared with nonathletic girls, being more likely to wait until they are at least seventeen to start being sexually active (54 percent versus 41 percent), being much less likely to have an unwanted pregnancy during high school (5 percent versus 11 percent), being three times more likely to graduate from high school, being less likely to have the kind of "hanging-out" time that is associated with getting into trouble, and having higher self-esteem and less depression.

All these findings are consistent with the idea that opening sports to girls is an effective way to help them cultivate physicality without limiting that physicality to sexuality and sensuality. It promises that girls' athletics can be a counterweight to social toxicity. Athletics teach a girl that there is more for her to do with her body than use it for sexual purposes. However, . . . the socially toxic forces at work in our society do not give up easily, and efforts are afoot to expropriate female athletes for socially toxic purposes. . . .

Sports Can Also Promote Aggressive Physicality

There are always side effects and unanticipated consequences of social change, even positive social change. When it comes to unleashing girls to be athletic, the costs mirror the benefits.

Gone wrong, involving girls in sports carries the same risks as involving boys does: The cultivation of physicality will translate into physical aggression.

Participation in rough-and-tumble sports can increase aggressive behavior. When Jeffrey Goldstein wrote his encyclopedic review *Aggression and Crimes of Violence,* he concluded that participation in athletic activities has a measurable effect on aggressive behavior, increasing it in proportion to the level of aggression contained within the particular sport engaged in. Contact sports like hockey, football, basketball, rugby, and soccer pose a greater risk than noncontact sports like tennis and golf. *Aggression is contagious.* This has led to the constant debate within educational, mental health, and coaching circles about how to prevent this aggression in the first place or, if that fails, how to contain it when it does occur. As we shall see, the role of adults as coaches and parents in defining the meaning of athletic experience is critical. Indeed, much of my concern for negative consequences is linked to the degree to which toxic adults are brought into the lives of girls through their participation in sports.

I read about and hear more and more accounts of sports-related physical aggression among girls. In Texas a middle school field hockey tournament ended in a knock-down, drag-out fight involving girls from both teams. According to a news story from Chicago headlined "Girls Suspended for Brawling After Volleyball Match," fighting broke out after a hotly contested game when players from the losing team followed the winning team into the locker room and started punching and kicking them. And here's nineteen-year-old Tiffany's account of another incident. She tells of her experience as a high school athlete in her hometown, a suburban community just outside St. Louis.

I was on the girls' varsity lacrosse team for three years. I guess when girls get aggressive, it's more personal than with boys. In our games the girls on the other teams used to go after our best players. My friend Jenny was one of the best players on our team. She used to get hit on the head at least three times each game—on purpose. The competition was less about the game and more about the individuals. The other team always did it when the referees weren't watching, so they wouldn't get penalties or get kicked out of the game. The girls did it because they wanted to hurt her. If she got hurt, she couldn't play, and she was our best player. I think they also did it because they were jealous of her. She was so good, and they weren't as good as she was.

Aggression May Be Linked to Psychology and Biology

Playing sports can bring out aggression. Most of this effect is psychological. The experience of rough-and-tumble sports models and reinforces physically aggressive behavior, such as crashing into people. That in turn tends to move to settings off the field, the court, and the diamond. That contagion seems clear. But more physiologically oriented researchers have also pointed to possible biological effects of sports. The links are complex, subtle, and somewhat controversial, but real nonetheless.

In a careful review of "Hormones and Sport: Behavior Effects of Androgen in Men and Women," published in the *Journal of Endocrinology*, neurobiologist K. [Kassandra] Christiansen reviews the evidence linking athletics to testosterone and aggression: "In humans, testosterone cannot elicit violence. It can only alter the probability that aggression is shown in a particular situation under a specific combination of external and internal cues." This is consistent with our own ecological perspective. If the question is, "Does testosterone cause increased aggression?," the answer is, of course, "It depends."

Second, high levels of testosterone in childhood are found to be associated with "physical aggressiveness and intense energy expenditures (vigorous play) but not verbal aggression," and these childhood patterns show up in adolescence. Whether or not this early pattern of rough-and-tumble play becomes the pathway to physical aggressiveness depends upon how it is received in the social environment of the child.

Third, "Regardless of the kind of sport, maximal or submaximal exercise (5–30 min) normally results in significant increases in testosterone levels. . . ." Involving kids in athletics engages them in this kind of exercise, with corresponding effects on hormone production and metabolism.

Finally, "several studies have shown that assertive or aggressive behavior followed by a rise in status levels leads to an increase in testosterone levels." Also, "The experience of winning and a rise in status even seems to maintain an already elevated level, sustaining the winner's activation and readiness to enter subsequent competition for higher status." It would appear from these studies that the more the athletic experience is tied to competition, the more likely it is to produce the testosterone-aggression link. As girls participate more in competitive athletic activities, their testosterone will rise, and thus they will become more likely to resort to aggression when they become aroused by anger or frustration "in the heat of the game." . . .

Competitive Sports Have Become Examples of Violence

But the potential links between competition and aggression are troubling, particularly in a social climate in which much of the athletic experience of girls is more and more organized around competition and winning. It's not too big a stretch to assert that cooperation breeds kindness; competition breeds hostility. This is part of what [Vietnamese zen Buddhist monk] Thich Nhat Hanh means when he speaks of experiences that water the seeds of compassion versus those of violence. It takes enlightened adult supervision and leadership to water the seeds of compassion on the playing field. Evidence is this is in short supply in our society.

"Progress" in Women's Basketball Comes with Rough Play

[July 22, 2008's] bench-clearing scuffle between the Los Angeles Sparks and Detroit Shock proved women can be just as boneheaded as men in the thick of intense athletic competition. . . .

The fight, which, by the way, isn't the WNBA's [Women's National Basketball Association's] first, showed that squaring up isn't a man thing. It's a sports thing. It's an athlete thing. . . .

In real life, athletes lose their tempers and use bad language. They're flawed. Female athletes aren't an exception.

Jemele Hill,
"In Real Life, Female Athletes Lose Their Temper, Too,"
www.espn.com Page 2, July 25, 2008.

Consider the June 7, 2004, issue of *U.S. News & World Report*. The cover story is entitled "Rescuing Children's Games from Crazed Coaches and Parents." And who is on the cover? A little girl in a baseball uniform, playing the infield, her expression one of intense resolve.

The article chronicles the toxicity of today's organized sports for kids. These include violent parental behavior toward children, coaches, or officials; 84 percent of parents said they had witnessed this. They include kids' being called names, yelled at, or insulted while playing; 45 percent of kids reported this. They include kids' being hit, kicked, or slapped while participating; 18 percent of kids reported this. There are also reports of rising numbers of sports-related injuries among children. Of course all this is happening in the lives of children in counterpoint with the bad behavior of professional athletes as watched by children on television, which includes everything from televised brawls during basketball, football, hockey, and baseball games to widespread steroid abuse.

There is also evidence of more and more intense competition starting earlier and earlier, with the rise of "traveling teams" that select the cream of the crop of children as young as eight for enhanced competition. The intensity of all this competitiveness is mirrored by the rise of a positive backlash, most notably in the form of the National Alliance for Youth Sports founded by Fred Engh (author of *Why Johnny Hates Sports*) and by the Women's Sports Foundation. Competition in athletics is a risky business, as Christiansen's review of the neurobiological evidence makes clear. I think the overall effect of girls in sports is overwhelmingly positive. But this does not mean we can or should ignore the physiological and the psychological risks. By acknowledging them, we can deal with them....

Revitalizing Sports' Positive Influences on Girls

Girls are not immune to the aggressive contagion effect of competitive sports. The biology of competition and aggression knows no absolute gender boundaries. Certainly their traditional roles and attitudes have shielded girls from these links historically, but that is changing. It's up to coaches and parents to minimize the toxic side effects of physical competition. How? By using athletics as a vehicle for teaching character. The best coaches and parents have always done this.

So what's the bottom line when it comes to the benefits and costs of unleashing girls from traditional "feminine" attitudes toward physical aggression? The new freedom and assertiveness experienced by girls can boost self-esteem and self-confidence. It can replace traditional problems of depression and self-doubt with buoyant confidence. It can offer girls who are different a positive way to be so. It can displace self-destruction to more healthy forms of coping. These all are positive changes, and we should welcome them.

At the same time we know that these positive changes are not the only changes, and we know that while they may be beneficial for most girls most of the time, there is a potential dark side to all this. We need to worry about what happens when girls are unleashed from the strictures of traditional femininity but are left to deal with social toxicity without experiences and training that prepare them to be sufficiently resilient.

> *"Girls who engaged in high school sports were more likely than were those who did not to have completed college 6 years after graduating from high school."*

Sports Participation Increases Rates of Female College Graduation

Kelly P. Troutman and Mikaela J. Dufur

Kelly P. Troutman, a former high school soccer player, teaches sociology at West Chester University in Pennsylvania; Mikaela J. Dufur is a faculty member of the department of sociology at Brigham Young University in Utah. In the following viewpoint, the authors assess the relationship between girls' participation in high school sports programs and their graduation from college. When all variables have been accounted for—including socioeconomic status, family dynamics, and race—high school female athletes are far more likely to obtain bachelor's degrees within six years of graduation from high school. No other extracurricular activity has the same effect.

Kelly P. Troutman and Mikaela J. Dufur, "From High School Jocks to College Grads: Assessing the Long-Term Effects of High School Sport Participation on Females' Educational Attainment," *Youth & Society*, vol. 38, June 2007, pp. 443–62. Copyright © 2007 Sage Publications. Reproduced by permission of Sage Publications.

As you read, consider the following questions:

1. When only sports participation is taken into consideration, how do the odds of college graduation increase with high school sport participation, according to the authors?

2. What other variables do the authors name that are associated with a girl's likelihood of graduating from college?

3. In the authors' view, what facts about girls and sports should be considered during conversations about educational policies and funding?

Numerous studies centered on high school athletics have demonstrated that participants in interscholastic sport enjoy various positive benefits from their involvement. Although some investigations have examined long-term implications and effects of high school sport participation, they tend to ignore female athletes. Because women's increased participation in high school sport is a relatively recent development, exploding during the past 30 years in part because of legislative intervention designed to provide more opportunities for women, investigations may now begin to look at whether the positive effects of women's sport participation persist or dissipate over time. In this article, we examine the long-term effects of high school sport participation on females' postsecondary educational attainment. . . .

Girls Find Unique Benefits in Sports Participation

Studies examining the postsecondary educational effects of participation in high school sport have found that athletic participation is positively related to college attendance and educational attainment. A problem with many of these studies, however, is that they have neglected including females in their sample. Given the small percentage of women participating in sport in many of the samples used, it is not surprising that women were excluded. In 1971 only 7.5% of high school athletes were female. This percentage has increased dramatically during the past few decades, and in 1996 girls made up approximately 40.0% of high school athletes. The change in the number of females engaging in interscholastic sport has largely been attributed to Title IX of the Education Amendments of 1972, which prohibited any institution receiving federal funding from practicing gender discrimination in educational programs or activities. The large increase in the number of females participating in sport has led to numerous investigations on athletic participation's effect on females. Recent studies have discovered that adolescent girls involved in sport experience some unique benefits.

Female adolescent athletes have been found to enjoy benefits related to mental health, self-confidence, and academic achievement. [Susan] Gore, [Florence] Farrell, and [Jennifer] Gordon's analysis found that participation in team sports helped protect girls, but not boys, with low GPAs [grade point averages] from depression. [Sandra L.] Hanson and [Rebecca S.] Kraus's investigation revealed that female sport participation was positively related to success in science, math, and engineering in the participants' sophomore and senior years of high school. This finding was not true of male athletes. Instead, boys' involvement in sport either had no effect or a negative effect on success in these subjects. Female athletes have also been found to be more achievement oriented, independent, self-confident, and inner controlled than their nonparticipating female counterparts. These findings suggest that athletic participation has considerable benefits for females at time of involvement. Whether women continue to enjoy these benefits later in life is largely unknown.

Although all of these benefits are worthy of investigation, this study centers on the relationship between female high school athletic participation and college completion because of relatively recent increases in both. In 1971, 13.8% of women between the ages of 25 and 29 had bachelor's degrees; by 1996, this percentage had risen to 28.2%, surpassing males by 2.0%. Although there is evidence of a relationship between females' former inter-scholastic sport involvement and college attendance, the question of whether these women are more likely to graduate from college remains. . . .

What the Statistics Reveal

Approximately 42% of high school females in our sample participated in interscholastic sport in 10th and/or 12th grade. On average, girls who engaged in high school sports were more likely than were those who did not to have completed college 6 years after graduating from high school.

Consistent with past research, students (in this particular case, females) involved in sport report higher educational expectations than those who are not involved and, on average, scored higher on standardized math and reading tests. White females were the most likely to participate in sport, with the percentage of White participants surpassing nonparticipants by 11%. Similar patterns did not occur for any other racial group. Hispanic and Black females were actually less likely to be involved in sport, and for Asians there was no difference between the two groups. In terms of family background characteristics, female athletes were more likely to come from families with a higher SES [socioeconomic status] and to live with both parents. Female athletes were also more likely to attend private school and schools in suburban or rural neighborhoods. . . .

Females' involvement in interscholastic high school sport is positively related to attainment of a bachelor's degree. The odds of college completion among females who played high school sport are 73% higher than the odds of college completion among females who did not engage in interscholastic sports. According to this analysis, college completion varies by school.

When all individual-level variables are controlled for, the effect of participation in high school sport on college completion decreases by 32% but retains its significance. The odds of college completion among females who participated in high school sport are still 42% higher than the odds of college completion among nonparticipating females when influential individual-level variables, such as SES, are controlled.

Various individual-level control variables help further explain factors associated with females' educational attainment. Not surprisingly, educational expectations had the greatest positive effect on females' college completion. The odds of women expecting to earn a bachelor's degree or higher actually doing so 6 years after high school were 4.4 times higher than the odds of women with lower educational expectations after controlling for the effects of all other variables in the model. Likewise, composite standardized test scores, SES, living with both parents, and participating in intercollegiate sports had a strong, positive relationship with college completion. The odds of Asians graduating from college were more than 2 times the odds of Whites graduating, whereas the odds of Hispanics and Native Americans graduating were 23% lower than those for Whites after controlling for all other variables in the model. Black females' odds of college completion were also higher than were those for Whites by about 37%. This finding is likely a result of our particular sample and the fact that Black college attendees with similar levels of prior educational achievement complete college at rates equal to or higher than White college students. Also, in more recent investigations where background differences are controlled for, Black females have been found to achieve more schooling than Whites. Interestingly, family size was found to be an insignificant predictor of women's attainment of a bachelor's degree.

College completion still appears to vary across schools, although the significance of the variance of the intercept decreases with the inclusion of these variables. . . .

When all individual-level and school-level background variables are controlled for, participation in high school sport still significantly affects the odds of college completion. In this analysis, the odds of graduating from college in 6 years are 41% higher for females who played inter-scholastic sport than the odds of college completion among females who did not engage in high school athletics. . . .

Sports Participation Is the Greatest Indicator

Results from this sample of females provide evidence that supports the hypothesis that females who played high school sport are more likely to graduate from college than are their counterparts. Even though background characteristics played the most significant role in decreasing the effect of high school sport participation on college completion, the odds of former high school athletes obtaining a bachelor's degree 6 years after completing high school were still significantly higher than were those of nonathletes. The positive relationship between females' former high school athletic involvement and college completion is consistent with past research that has shown sport participation to be related to positive outcomes and more specifically on the relationship between athletics and academic success. As indicated by previous studies on the subject, there does not appear to be a zero-sum relationship between sport participation and educational achievement for girls.

The positive relationship found between females' former high school athletic involvement and college completion helps validate legislation mandating equal opportunities and funding for female sports. Although Title IX greatly contributed to the progression toward more equal athletic opportunities, fe-

Sport Participation Teaches Life Skills

Athletic participation is ... associated with responsible social behaviors, enhanced personal skills, and greater success in school. Female student-athletes learn important life skills, including the ability to work with a team, to perform under pressure, to set goals, and to take criticism. In addition, playing sports helps young women develop self-confidence, perseverance, dedication, and a competitive edge. Female student-athletes also have higher grades and higher high school graduation rates than their non-athletic peers. Athletic participation can also lead to college scholarships. ...

Female athletes of color also experience higher levels of self-esteem, are more likely to be involved in extracurricular activities, and are more likely to become leaders in their communities than girls of color who do not play sports. Female athletes of color get better grades than their non-athletic peers. In particular, African American female athletes are 15% more likely to graduate from college than their non-athletic peers.

National Women's Law Center and Harvard School of Public Health, Keeping Score: Girls' Participation in High School Athletics in Massachusetts, *2004.*

males in high school are still offered 8% fewer single-gender inter-scholastic sports than are boys, and only two states, which implemented additional state laws, have reached the actual parity threshold of Title IX. ...

Our findings ... suggest a societal benefit to female sport participation in the form of increased educational attainment. Given the importance of educational attainment in subsequent SES, and coupled with previous findings demonstrating other benefits to female participation in sports, the results of this study suggest that, rather than looking for ways to excuse schools from Title IX compliance, the federal government should join state and local efforts to promote equal athletic opportunities for female students.

Findings from this research are also useful for educational policy and the allocation of resources. America's education system is experiencing increased pressure to improve students' proficiency and standardized test scores, and in some instances, costly extracurricular activities have received reduced funds or been cut entirely. This analysis of sport's long-term educational effect on females should aid policy makers in their decisions regarding funding for interscholastic sport programs. Providing more opportunities for female participation in sport may help bring about positive academic changes. It is imperative that these opportunities be open to minority and low-income students who are less likely to participate in high school sports.

Although this study offers valuable insight on females' high school sport involvement as it relates to postsecondary education and current theoretical debate on the matter, some important considerations were not addressed that should be investigated in future research. For example, the effect of different types of sport (e.g., team vs. individual), level of involvement (junior varsity vs. varsity), years of participation, degree of commitment, and expectations of future involvement in sport on educational attainment have yet to be examined. It is possible that variations in these variables affect academic success differently. Future research might also aim to better understand how social capital in this activity differs from other extracurricular activities that do not produce the same academic benefits. In addition, previous research provides mixed evidence for whether male students' participation in sports provides the same benefits female students' participation does. Additional research into whether the long-term effects of sport participation for boys mirror those of girls or how the mechanism of sport participation might work differently for boys and girls is still needed.

Periodical Bibliography

The following articles have been selected to supplement the diverse views presented in this chapter.

Aimee Berg "Cradle of a Sport Has Crossed the Gender Line," *New York Times*, May 13, 2007.

Ryan J. Foley "Appeals Court: Boy Can't Compete on High School Girls' Team," Associated Press, November 30, 2006.

James Hannah "Crashing Through the Wall: NFL Player's Sister Defies Gender Roles as Varsity Lineman," *Grand Rapids Press*, August 25, 2007.

Gwen Knapp "Gender Bias Can Cut Both Ways," *San Francisco Chronicle*, May 27, 2008.

Rafiq Maqbool "Challenging Gender Barriers, Teen Girls in Afghanistan Enter Boxing Ring," Associated Press, November 16, 2007.

Jon Moffett "Pens Feel the Drive to Inspire," *Vindicator (Youngstown, OH)*, April 22, 2009.

Merryn Sherwood and Chris Dutton "Playing over the Gender Divide," *Canberra Times (Canberra, Australia)*, November 8, 2008.

Kara Spak "Middle School Girls Lead 'Second Wave of Feminism,'" *Chicago Sun-Times*, April 18, 2009.

Katie Thomas "Study Finds Gender Barrier in Sports," *New York Times*, October 9, 2008.

Greg Victor "Saturday Diary: In Praise of Swimming," *Pittsburgh Post-Gazette*, September 22, 2007.

Stephanie Walter, et al. "Does Participation in Organized Sports Predict Future Physical Activity for Adolescents from Diverse Economic Backgrounds?" *Journal of Adolescent Health*, March 2009.

For Further Discussion

Chapter 1

1. Men and women usually play on same-sex teams because of differences in the average size of adult males and females, which tend to favor men in competitions that rely on strength, speed, and size. Among boys and girls, however, the physical differences are fewer. After reading the viewpoints by Kris Lines and Sarah K. Fields, answer these questions: Why do you think boys and girls play on same-sex teams in older childhood and adolescence? What factors other than gender could be used to determine how to place young athletes on sports teams?

2. For thousands of years, competitive sports have been considered primarily the domain of men and boys. Over the past several decades, women and girls have been participating in increasingly larger numbers, despite criticisms—stated and implied—that sports would make them unfeminine or unattractive. Do you think girls playing sports are more scrutinized for gender behavior than boys are? To what degree are people surprised by girls' participation in sports? To what degree are they angered or threatened by it? Use the information presented in the viewpoints by Lisa A. Harrison and Amanda B. Lynch and by Deirdre M. Kelly and coauthors to discuss these questions.

3. Although girls and boys play some of the same sports in school, there are distinct versions of most of them, with different rules (such as in lacrosse) or different equipment (such as baseball vs. softball) as demonstrated in the viewpoints by Patricia Sanchez and Preston Williams. Do boys and girls demonstrate athleticism differently enough to require separate games or rules? What possible benefits

arise from distinguishing game play between boys' and girls' teams? Is it of any significance that most individual sports (such as track or swimming) are performed exactly the same way by males and females?

Chapter 2

1. Sports participation is often thought to be a source of high self-esteem in female athletes; girls learn to take pride in their accomplishments and benefit from the social structure that a team and coach provide, as Lindsay A. Taliaferro and coauthors show. According to David R. Shaffer and Erin Wittes, however, girls who do not enjoy playing sports may be negatively affected by being forced to participate (such as in gym class). Do sports offer psychological and social advantages to all participants? If girls do not enjoy playing sports, should they be taught other ways to maintain physical fitness or should teachers and coaches seek out different ways to present sports so they are more enjoyable?

2. Mike Perko, Todd Bartee, and Mike Dunn decry how frequently steroids and other "fitness supplements" are being marketed to girls, and they especially express concern about the reasons that girls are responding to such commercial campaigns. Gen Kanayama and coauthors, however, dispute the idea that girls are taking steroids in such great numbers, claiming that the surveys used poor methodology to gather information. Does it matter if girls only rarely consume anabolic-androgenic steroids if they seek them out and know they are taking them? Is the steroid issue in girls' sports a problem of behavior and perception, of actual medical danger, or of both?

Chapter 3

1. Even when schools administer policies to provide opportunities for girls to play sports in greater numbers and

with better facilities, results are slow to follow. What factors might be behind the delay between compliance with Title IX regulations and perfect gender equality in sports programs? Is a discrepancy the result of sexism? Is it possible to immediately implement and support girls' athletics programs to the same degree that support has been given to boys? What obstacles must be overcome? Use the viewpoints by Becky Vest and Gerald Masterson and by Megan Seely to inform your answers.

2. While the government has the power to affect availability of opportunity and funding for girls' participation in sports, laws cannot change attitudes or personal preferences, as shown in the viewpoint by Carrie Lukas. Are there gender differences in the interest in sports? Are these differences innate or culturally learned? Considering the information presented in the viewpoint by R. Vivian Acosta and Linda Jean Carpenter, what do you think the gender balance of boys and girls in sports programs will look like ten years from now? What about fifty years from now? Girls have always expressed interest in athleticism and participated in exercise. Has the term "sports" been too narrowly defined?

3. Consider the opinions and facts given in the viewpoints by Jon Siegel and Rob Stein. Controversy surrounds whether cheerleading can be counted as a sport if it is noncompetitive, and whether competitive cheerleading is still cheerleading. How much do these terms matter? If "cheerleading" were to be officially split into two different activities, would competitive sports cheerleaders get more financial support and school appreciation? Would cheering squad cheerleaders get better supervision and coaches with more training and skill? Should the designation of an activity as a sport (or not) determine the appropriate level of physical risk for participants?

Chapter 4

1. At advanced levels of competition, athletes often perform better when their ratio of muscle mass to total body weight is higher. Because girls' bodies gain fat tissue as part of the adolescent maturation process, girls often feel compelled to diet as one way to maintain their competitive edge, as shown by the viewpoints given by Eli Saslow and by A.P. (Karin) de Bruin and coauthors. Considering that school sports seasons only last a few months, should coaches be concerned about girls dieting? Does a coach have the right to counsel an athlete about weight, particularly a coach of a team sport? Are young athletes the best judges of when they are pushing themselves too far? Who should decide how hard athletes train?

2. Girls' participation in sports has been blamed and credited for many new aspects of girls' position in society, often in the sense that girls have taken their places beside boys for good or ill, as presented in the viewpoints by James Garbarino and by Kelly P. Troutman and Mikaela J. Dufur. If girls are approaching boys in general aggressiveness, is that a bad thing? Is aggression a skill or a character flaw? Would more aggressive girls result in a society of more aggressive women? Do aggressive women achieve more in their personal and professional lives? Do you think that advancements girls have made in higher education stem from sports training or other social factors?

Organizations to Contact

The editors have compiled the following list of organizations concerned with the issues debated in this book. The descriptions are derived from materials provided by the organizations. All have publications or information available for interested readers. The list was compiled on the date of publication of the present volume; the information provided here may change. Be aware that many organizations take several weeks or longer to respond to inquiries, so allow as much time as possible.

Canadian Association for the Advancement of Women and Sport and Physical Activity (CAAWS)
N202 - 801 King Edward Ave., Ottawa, ON K1N 6N5
   Canada
(613) 562-5667 • fax: (613) 562-5668
e-mail: caaws@caawss.ca
Web site: www.caaws.ca

CAAWS envisions an equitable sport and physical activity system in which Canadian girls and women have the right to all the benefits of participating in sport and physical activity and can participate as decision-makers and leaders. Towards these aims, CAAWS is an advocate for equity for girls and women in sport and physical activity and promotes the values of equity, inclusiveness, fairness, and respect. CAAWS publishes reports on a variety of topics related to this issue and sponsors special programs to reach women of many ages, interests, and ability levels.

Feminist Majority Foundation (FMF)
1600 Wilson Blvd., #801, Arlington, VA 22209
(703) 522-2214 • fax: (703) 522-2219
Web site: www.feminist.org/sports

The Feminist Majority Foundation believes a majority of men and women support the equality of women in all aspects of public and personal life, including athletics, and provides resources and support to empower them in their beliefs. The Gender Equity in Athletics and Sports division of the FMF provides information and policy recommendations about the inclusion of women and girls in sports, about the special needs and accomplishments of women athletes, and about the history and support of Title IX legislation as it relates to access to sports programs.

Girls on the Run International
120 Cottage Pl., Charlotte, NC   28207
Web site: www.girlsontherun.org

Girls on the Run is a nonprofit prevention program that encourages preteen girls to develop self-respect and healthy lifestyles through running. The curricula address all aspects of girls' development: their physical, emotional, mental, social, and spiritual well-being. The organization's objective is to reduce the potential of at-risk activities among its participants, with a goal of fewer adolescent pregnancies, eating disorders, instances of depression, and suicide attempts, as well as fewer substance/alcohol abuse problems and confrontations with the juvenile justice system. There are more than 150 local chapters across the United States and Canada.

International Working Group on Women and Sport (IWG)
IWG Secretariat, University of Technology
Sydney, NSW 2070
  Australia
Web site: www.iwg-gti.org

The IWG was established in 1994 at the first World Conference on Women and Sport in Australia. It is an independent coordinating body consisting of representatives of key government and nongovernmental organizations from different regions of the world, primarily funded and supported by groups in the United Kingdom, Namibia, Canada, Japan, and Australia. Its vision is to realize a sustainable sporting culture that enables and values the full involvement of women in every aspect of sport, globally. It publishes a quarterly newsletter and hosts an international conference on women and sport every four years.

National Association of Collegiate Women Athletics Administrators (NACWAA)

5018 Randall Parkway, #3, Wilmington, NC   28403
(910) 793-8244 • fax: (910) 793-8246
Web site: www.nacwaa.org

The NACWAA is an organization dedicated to providing educational programs, professional and personal development opportunities, information exchange, and support services to enhance college athletics and to promote the growth, leadership, and success of women as athletics administrators, professional staff, coaches, and student-athletes. Its purpose is to provide a forum for discussion, interaction, and information exchange among individuals confronted by similar challenges that affect and influence collegiate athletics, particularly as they relate to women student-athletes and women collegiate administrators. The NACWAA hosts an annual national convention for its members and publishes a quarterly newsletter.

Tucker Center for Research on Girls and Women in Sport

University of Minnesota, 203 Cooke Hall
Minneapolis, MN   55455
(612) 625-7327
e-mail: info@tuckercenter.org
Web site: www.cehd.umn.edu/tuckercenter

Housed at the University of Minnesota, the Tucker Center is an interdisciplinary research center leading an effort to examine how sport and physical activity affect the lives of girls and women, their families, and communities. It focuses on scholarship that directly impacts the physical activity experience of and for girls and women and researches how sport and physical activity improve girls and women's psychosocial and physical health throughout their lives—promoting girls' self-confidence, preventing eating disorders, or helping women stay healthy as they age. It hosts a lecture series and publishes a newsletter each spring and fall semester.

Women Talk Sports

Web site: www.womentalksports.com

WomenTalkSports.com is an online network that connects blogs relating to women's sports. The site aims to raise the level of awareness of women in sport by providing comprehensive sport coverage, spotlighting outstanding achievements, and working with sporting associations on advocacy issues and empowering programs. Its goal is to promote and empower female athleticism. The site serves as a calendar of events, library of articles, women and girls' camp and league contact information, and a collection of links to other Web sites about women's sports. It is a dedicated platform for women to exchange ideas, debate, and engage each other.

Women Win

Saxen Weirmarlaan 20-3, CB Amsterdam   1075
   The Netherlands
e-mail: info@womenwin.org
Web site: www.womenwin.org

Women Win is an international women's fund that supports sport and physical activity as instruments for social change and women's empowerment. Its members believe sport is a way for women and girls to learn leadership skills and to develop character, self-esteem, and a sense of belonging, while discovering the fun, support, and power of being together. Women Win's objectives are to support innovative and sustainable sports programs for women and girls and to advocate for and create a social movement using sport to achieve gender equality. The fund awards grants to women's organizations and individuals who design projects in line with its goals.

Women's Sport and Fitness Foundation UK (WSFF)
3rd Fl., Victoria House, Bloomsbury Square
London   WC18 4SE
e-mail: info@wsff.org.uk
Web site: www.wsf.org.uk

The WSFF believes in a society that encourages, enables, and celebrates active women and girls. Its goals are to make sport as appealing to women and girls as it is to boys, make women and girls aware of the importance of being active, and make fit and healthy women and girls social and cultural role models. The organization conducts research and partners with government organizations and with business and media outlets to inform the public and influence policy at the highest social and political levels. The WSFF publishes a variety of reports and hosts an annual conference.

Women's Sports Foundation (WSF)
Eisenhower Park, 1899 Hempstead Turnpike, #400
East Meadow, NY   11554
(516) 542-4700 • fax: (516) 542-4716
e-mail: info@womenssportsfoundation.org
Web site: www.womenssportsfoundation.org

Founded in 1974 by Billie Jean King, the Women's Sports Foundation is a national charitable and educational organization dedicated to advancing the lives of girls and women through physical activity. The WSF has a rich history of conducting important research and has made a long-term commitment to a series of signature reports addressing such topics as girls' participation in sports and physical activity, gender equity in intercollegiate sports, the impact of media images of women in sports, and pay equity. One of the main activities of the WSF is the GoGirlGo! initiative to get one million inactive girls to participate in regular physical activity and to keep another million already active girls from stopping.

Bibliography of Books

Christine A. Baker — *Why She Plays: The World of Women's Basketball.* Lincoln, NE: University of Nebraska Press, 2008.

Gale Bernhardt — *Bicycling for Women.* Boulder, CO: VeloPress, 2008.

Madeleine Blais — *In These Girls, Hope Is a Muscle.* New York: Atlantic Monthly Press, 1995.

Katie Brown — *Girl on the Rocks: A Woman's Guide to Climbing with Strength, Grace, and Courage.* Guilford, CT: Falcon Guides, 2008.

Marilyn Cohen — *No Girls in the Clubhouse: The Exclusion of Women from Baseball.* Jefferson, NC: McFarland, 2009.

Tim Dahlberg, Mary Ederle Ward, and Brenda Greene — *America's Girl: The Incredible Story of How Swimmer Gertrude Ederle Changed the Nation.* New York: St. Martin's Press, 2009.

Terry Eguaoje — *Bridging the Gender Gap in Sports Leadership: An Evaluation of Female Soccer Coaches.* Mustang, OK: Tate Publishing, 2008.

Janet Eveleigh — *The Girl's Guide to Action Sports: Everything You Need to Know to Get Started—In Style!* London: A & C Black Publishers, 2009.

Shelley Frost — *Throw Like a Girl: Discovering the Body, Mind and Spirit of the Athlete in You!* Hillsboro, OR: Beyond Words Publishing, 2000.

Ilse Hartman-Tews and Gertrud Pfister, eds. — *Sport and Women: Social Issues in International Perspective.* New York: Routledge/ISCPES, 2003.

Ron Hotchkiss — *The Matchless Six: The Story of Canada's First Women's Olympic Team.* Toronto: Tundra Books, 2006.

Lisa Leslie and Larry Burnett — *Don't Let the Lipstick Fool You: The Making of a Champion.* New York: Kensington Publishing Group, 2008.

Michael A. Messner — *It's All for the Kids: Gender, Families, and Youth Sports.* Berkeley, CA: University of California Press, 2009.

Jean O'Reilly and Susan K. Cahn, eds. — *Women and Sports in the United States.* Boston: Northeastern University Press, 2007.

Linda Peavy and Ursula Smith — *Full Court Quest: The Girls from Fort Shaw Indian School Basketball Champions of the World.* Norman, OK: University of Oklahoma Press, 2008.

Jennifer Ring — *Stolen Bases: Why American Girls Don't Play Baseball.* Urbana, IL: University of Illinois Press, 2009.

Patty Segovia and Rebecca Heller — *Skater Girl: A Girl's Guide to Skateboarding.* Berkeley, CA: Ulysses Press, 2007.

Monica Seles — *Getting a Grip: On My Body, My Mind, My Self.* New York: Avery, 2009.

Jennifer Sey — *Chalked Up: Inside Elite Gymnastics' Merciless Coaching, Overzealous Parents, Eating Disorders, and Elusive Olympic Dreams.* New York: William Morrow, 2008.

Welch Suggs — *A Place on the Team: The Triumph and Tragedy of Title IX .* Princeton, NJ: Princeton University Press, 2005.

Anne M. Todd — *Venus and Serena Williams: Athletes.* New York: Chelsea House, 2009.

Kate Torgovnick — *Cheer!: Inside the Secret World of College Cheerleaders.* New York: Touchstone, 2008.

Carlos Velez, III — *En Garde!: A Girl's Introduction to the World of Fencing.* Terre Haute, IN: Wish Publishing, 2008.

Robert K. Wallace — *Thirteen Women Strong: The Making of a Team.* Lexington, KY: University Press of Kentucky, 2008.

Susan Ware — *Title IX: A Brief History with Documents.* Boston: Bedford/St. Martin's, 2007.

Patricia Campbell Warner — *When the Girls Came Out to Play: The Birth of American Sportswear.* Amherst, MA: University of Massachusetts Press, 2006.

Index